THEN & NOW

PLANT CITY

OPPOSITE: In this photograph taken sometime after 1914, looking southwest across town from the water tower, Warnell Lumber and Veneer Company's mills are seen in the left background. Baker Street had not yet been extended east across the tracks. This view clearly defines what was considered to be the limit for the incorporated city.

THEN & NOW

PLANT CITY

Shelby Jean Roberson Bender
and Roberta Donaldson Jordan

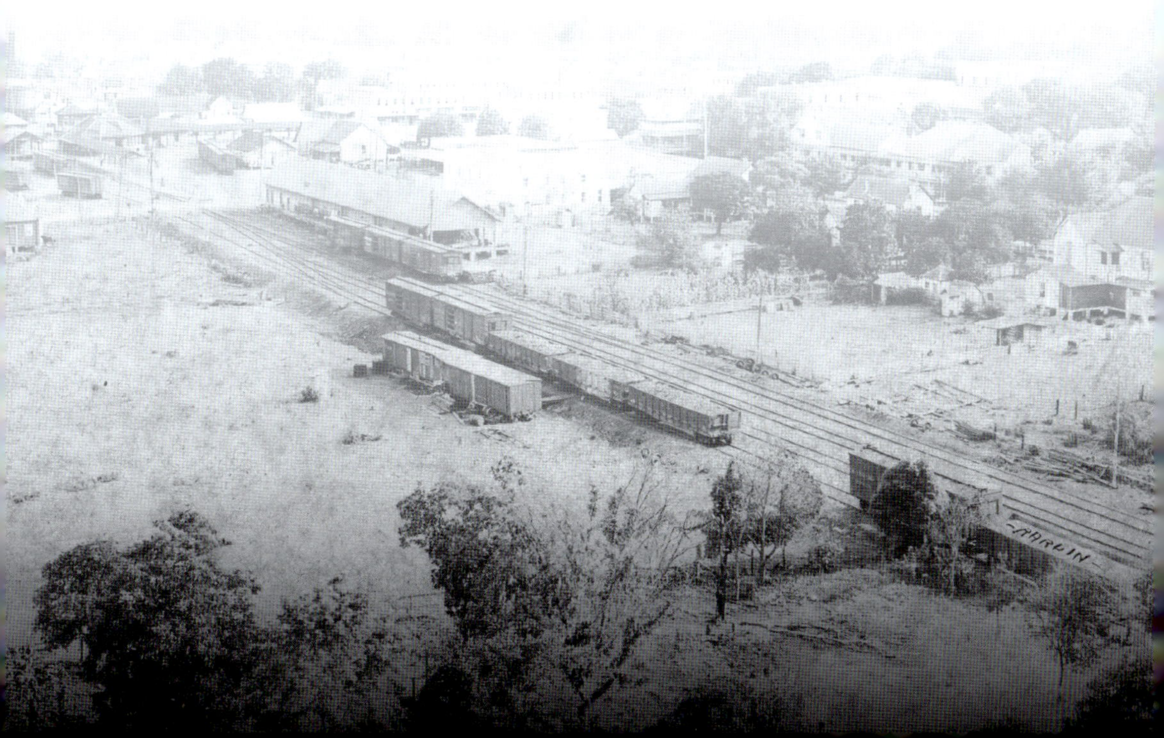

For our family and friends who have given us the support and encouragement to continue our endeavor of recording Plant City's history, both then and now. Although history is past, it is ever present and changing.

ISBN 978-0-7385-8748-6

Library of Congress Control Number: 2010937738

Published by Arcadia Publishing
Charleston, South Carolina

Printed in the United States of America

For all general information, please contact Arcadia Publishing:
Telephone 843-853-2070
Fax 843-853-0044
E-mail sales@arcadiapublishing.com
For customer service and orders:
Toll-Free 1-888-313-2665

Visit us on the Internet at www.arcadiapublishing.com

On the Front Cover: City hall is the downtown location for local government services. The current city hall, built of redbrick with column trim, was designed as a reminder of the 1923 stately Georgian-style building, as photographed in 1950.

On the Back Cover: A roadside directional sign welcomed and enticed visitors to the city that has long been known as the "Winter Strawberry Capital of the World."

Contents

Acknowledgments

To capture a picture of our gratitude towards all those persons, then and now, who have helped bring this publication to fruition would be impossible. There would be no *now*, if not for *then*. We all have great memories of how things were in the past, and for this we know that we must continue to record our history for the generations to come. Our interest and dedication to "Preserving the Past for the Future," the motto of the East Hillsborough Historical Society (EHHS), of which we have both given many years of volunteer service to, make up the underlying support for this publication. The EHHS, a 501c3 formed in 1974, is dedicated to the preservation of the historical and cultural heritage of Plant City and eastern Hillsborough County. The Quintilla Geer Bruton Archives Center is the genealogy and history library, and the Pioneer Museum includes exhibits of Plant City's early days and development. The Archives Center, Pioneer Museum, and offices of the society are located in the 1914 Plant City High School, a National Register of Historic Places site owned by the City of Plant City and operated under partnership with the East Hillsborough Historical Society. The authors' other Arcadia publications include Images of America: *Plant City*, *Plant City in Vintage Postcards*, and Postcards of America: *Plant City's Berry Season*. The success of these publications has provided us the encouragement to present to you Then & Now: *Plant City*.

All images appear courtesy of the East Hillsborough Historical Society.

—Shelby Jean Roberson Bender and Roberta Donaldson Jordan, coauthors

Introduction

"I remember then" . . . how often do we hear this statement? Many times we think of the past when focusing on where we are now. Plant City is more than its buildings. The structures are just the shell or the outline; it is the people who tell the story.

Plant City's story begins with Henry B. Plant. His 1883 extension of the South Florida Railroad into the Central Florida area known as Ichepuckesassa brings us to today. The trains still come through town, any hour of the day and in all directions. The passenger trains do not stop here anymore, but residents can wave to them as their cars pass by.

Early settlers who came to the area in the 1830s lived just north of the current downtown. These pioneers literally left their mark on this community. Our streets and buildings bear their names and serve as a reminder of how past history has made a difference in the Plant City community of today. In 1884, the *Plant City Courier*, our local newspaper, was established. One hundred twenty-six years later, we are still reading the *Courier*, a weekly newspaper covering our community's current events. Plant City incorporated as a town on January 10, 1885. Land sold at desirable prices, attracting newcomers to town. Cattle, vegetables, and citrus were joined by the cotton and lumber businesses as rail freight was made available.

Strawberries were brought here in the early 1880s from Shannon, Mississippi, and in Plant City the strawberry is still king.

Both the beginning and end of the 20th century brought change to our town. Military service, a commitment to excellence in education, and dedication to our family through social and religious foundation has always played an important role in the life of Plant City. Neighborhoods were built and businesses were formed.

Plant City has both a history and a future. From a single square-mile town with a population of 300 to a community of almost 30,000 people, change has been inevitable. Electricity, telephone, and automobiles were big news in the early 20th century. As we embrace and move forward in the 21st century, technology has become the key. Plant City is still a town of brick streets with granite curbs. We have changed the way we live, work, and play, and reflecting upon those visions is how we present Then & Now: *Plant City*. For a closer look, please also enjoy reading Arcadia's other Plant City publications—Images of America: *Plant City*, *Plant City in Vintage Postcards*, and Postcards of America: *Plant City's Berry Season*.

CHAPTER 1

CITY HISTORY AND GOVERNMENT

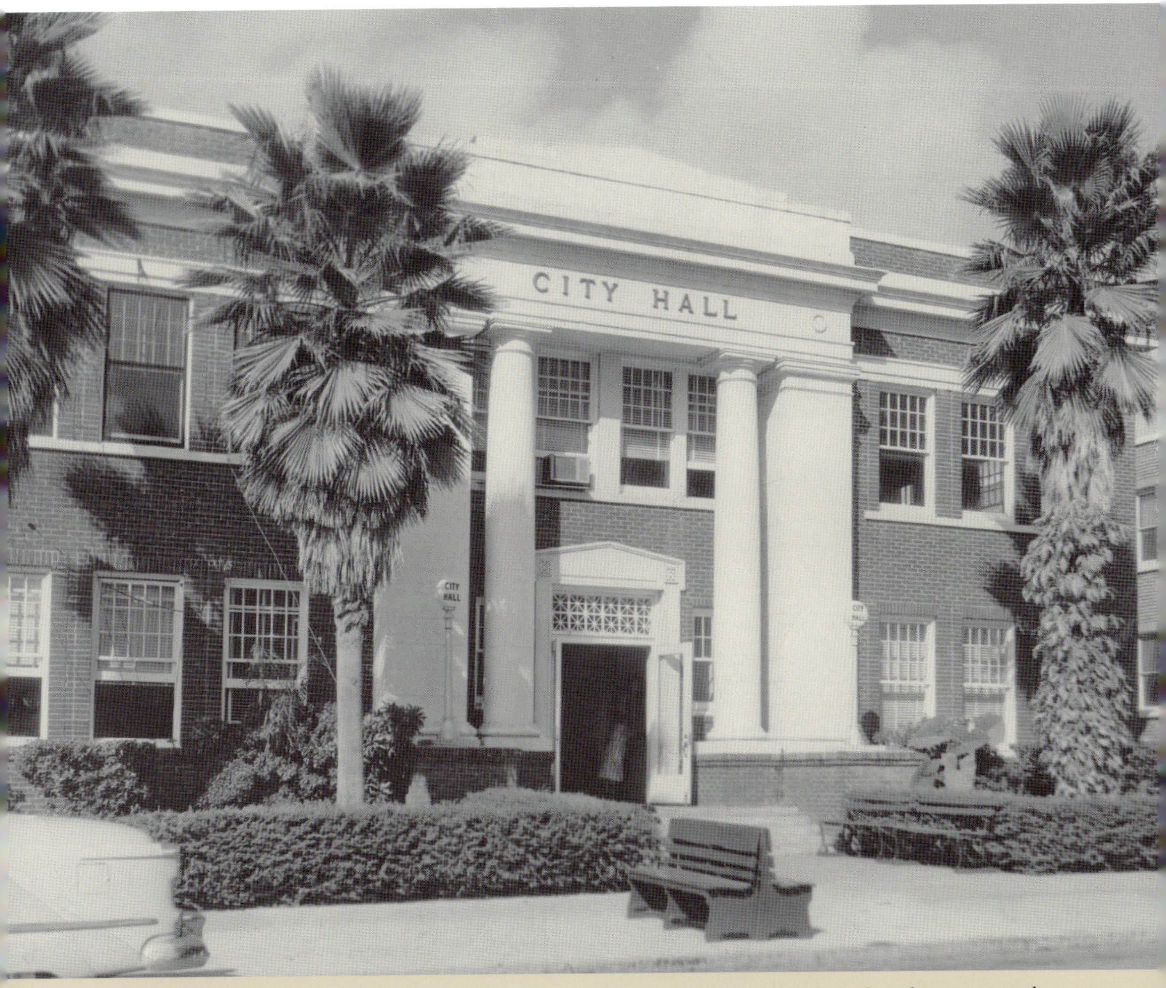

This is an early 1950s photograph of the city hall building located at the northwest corner of Collins and Palmer Streets. The property was sold to the First Baptist Church in 1959 when the city erected a new building at the northwest corner of Wheeler and Mahoney Streets.

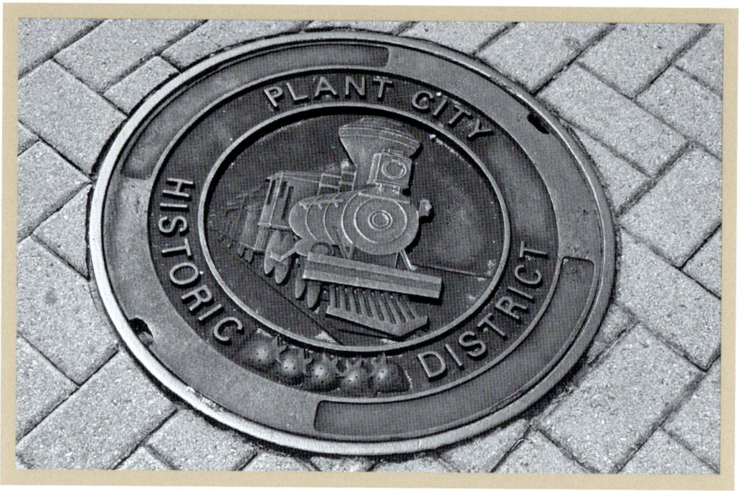

Plant City's development is attributed to the 1883 extension of Henry B. Plant's South Florida Railroad into the Central Florida area referred to as Ichepuckesassa, now known as Plant City. The city is crisscrossed by train tracks, and one can hear the whistle blowing while strolling the downtown streets. Plant City has three local and national registered historic districts. Cast-iron markers with strawberries and trains compliment the crosswalks of the granite-curbed brick streets.

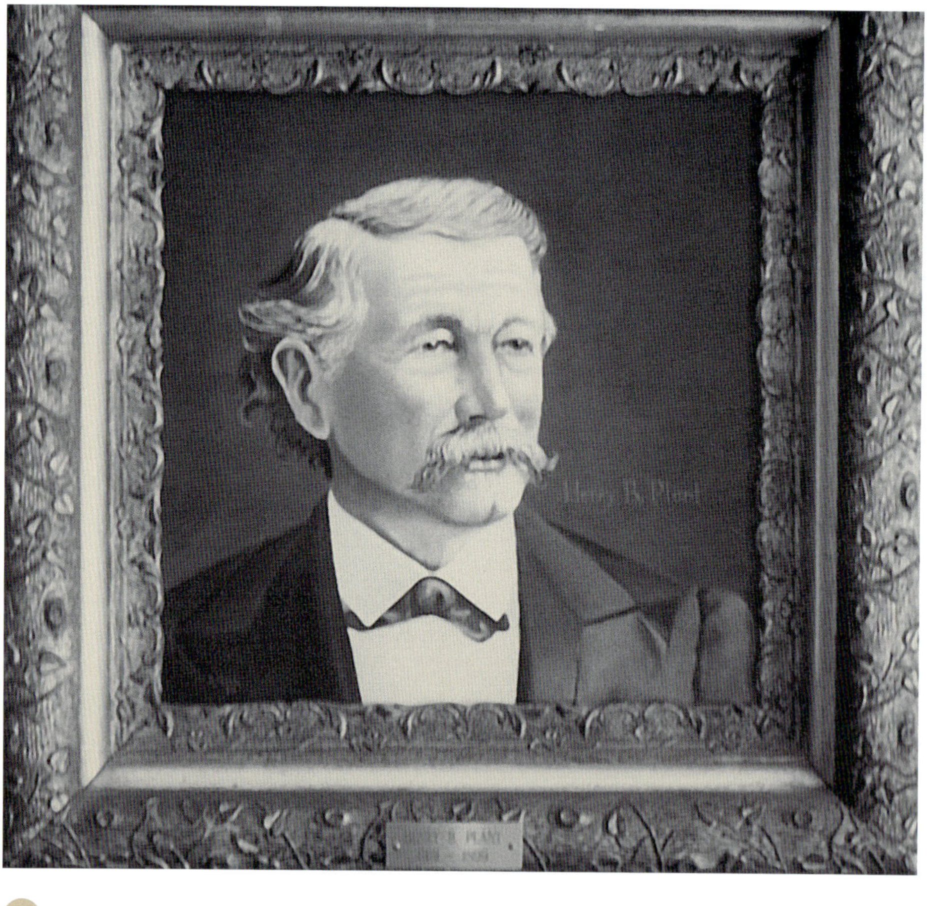

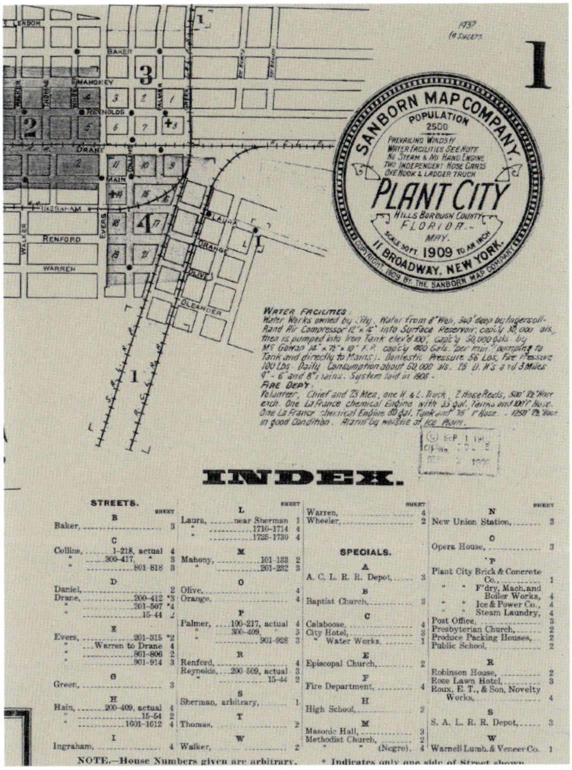

According to the 1909 Sanborn Map Company, the population of Plant City totaled 2,500. The fire department was 23 comprised of volunteer men, and the alarm was at the local ice plant. The daily water consumption of 60,000 gallons was from a system installed in 1908. The 1960s aerial view below of a portion of the early downtown footprint shows churches, homes, and businesses, as well as the 1959 city hall. Only the two church structures remain on their original sites, as change has brought about other uses in this downtown area.

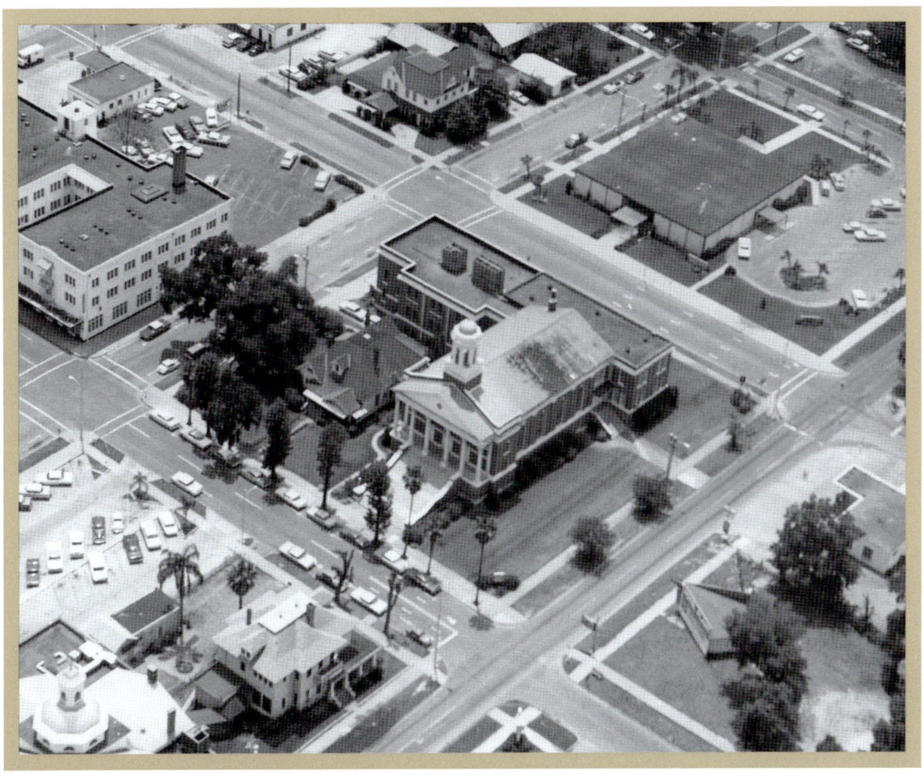

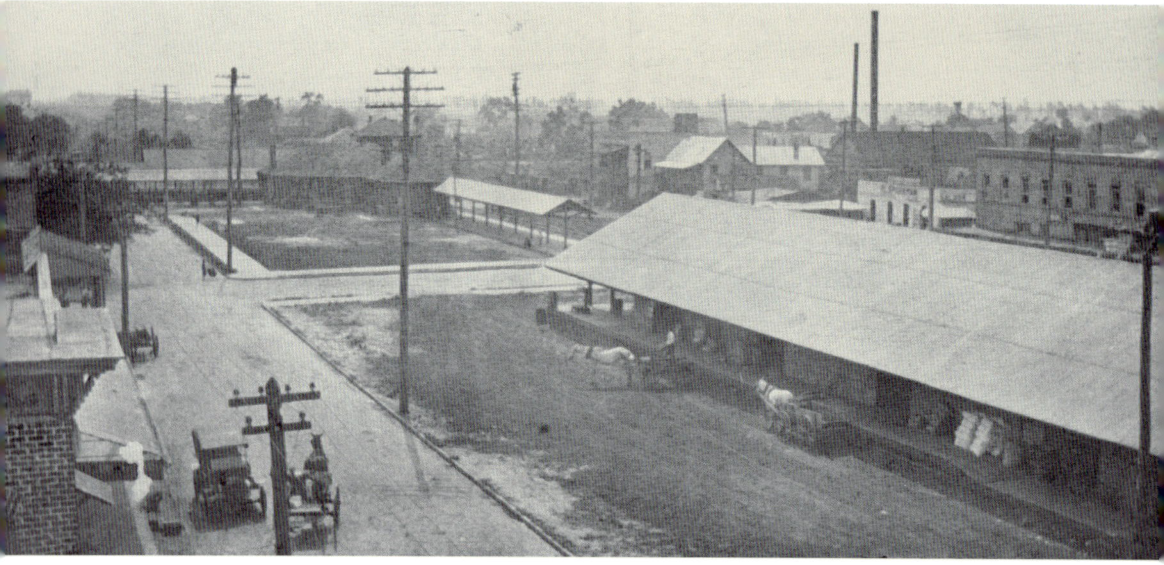

Local farmers and growers brought their crops to town in their horse-drawn wagons. In the early image of downtown, only a single motorcar is seen, with the railway depot and Union Station in the background. The current photograph shows the depot as the Plant City Welcome Center. The monthly motorcycle and car shows, as well as other outdoor events, are held here.

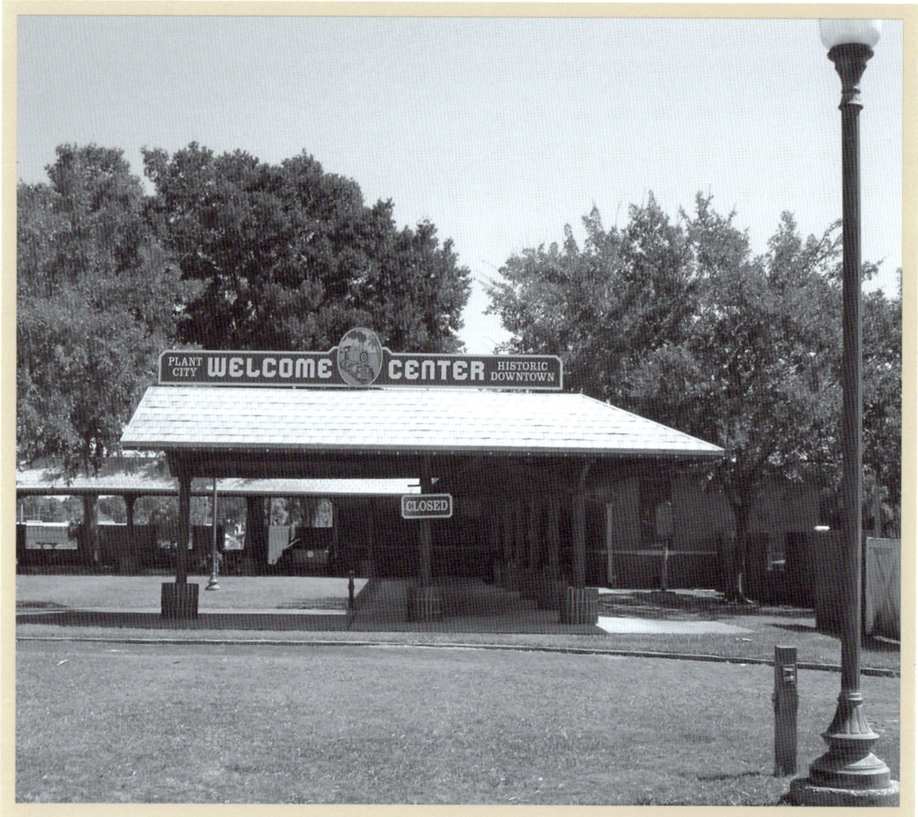

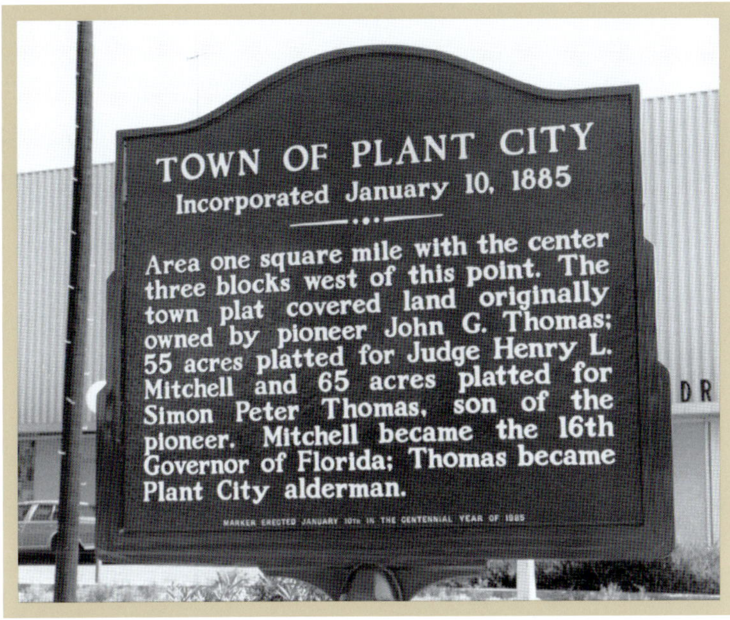

Shortly after the incorporation of Plant City as a town in January 1885, the Methodist people of the community relocated from the Shiloh area and constructed their first church building on Haines Street (now Dr. Martin Luther King Jr. Boulevard) near the intersection of South Howard Street. In 1985, Plant City celebrated its centennial year and erected a new marker adjacent to the railway line at South Collins Street and J. Arden Mays Boulevard. Plant City is no longer a single square-mile town.

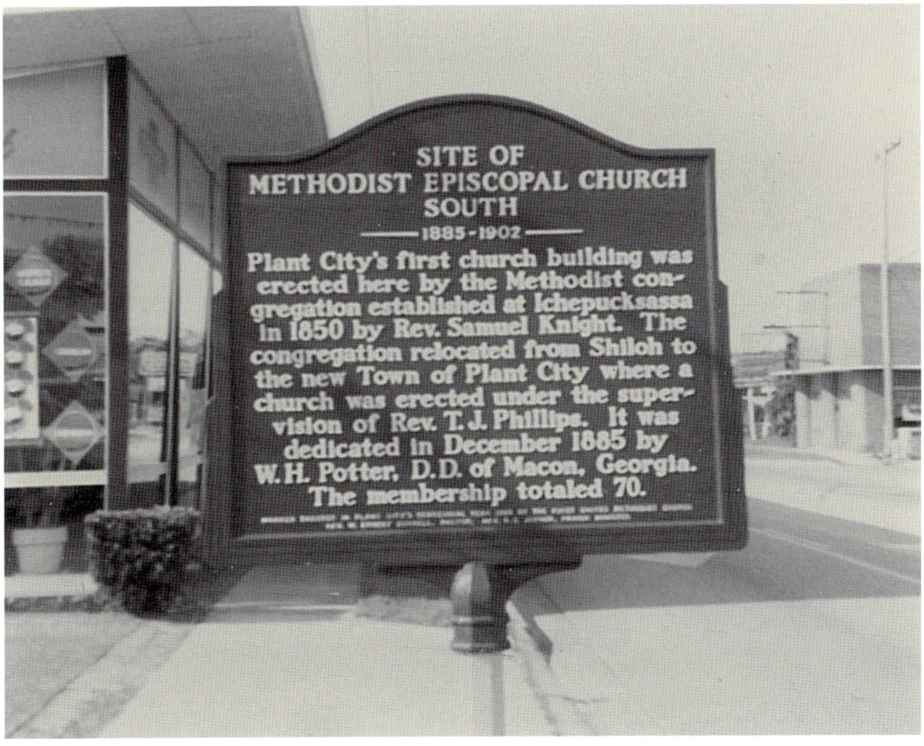

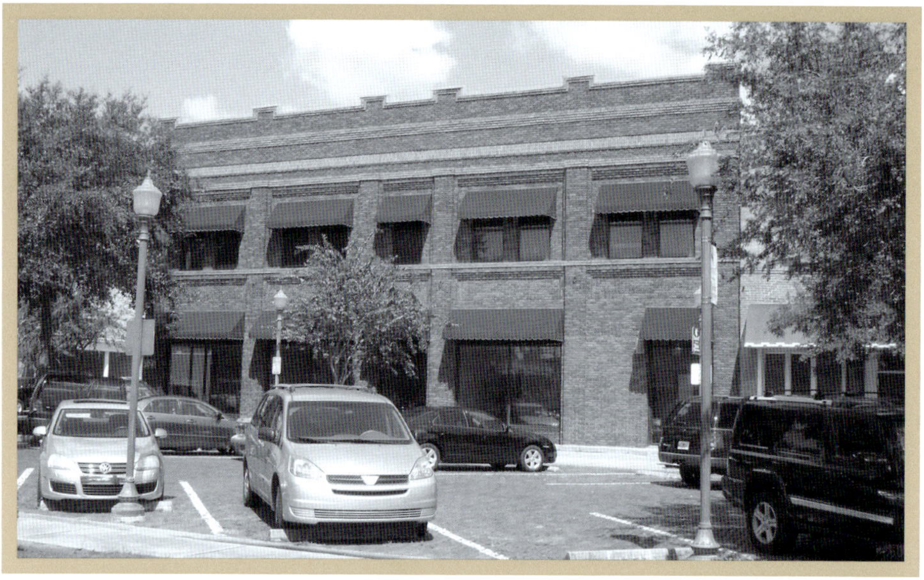

The 1915 fire, which was believed to have been caused by an arsonist, destroyed the Mays Building at the corner of North Drane and Evers Streets. The Opera House, located on the third floor, was the site of the Plant City High School commencement exercises. Owner Wells and Sons Company erected a new two-story building, as seen in the current photograph. Historical-style street lamps were added during a recent downtown revitalization, complimenting the original brick streets and granite curbs.

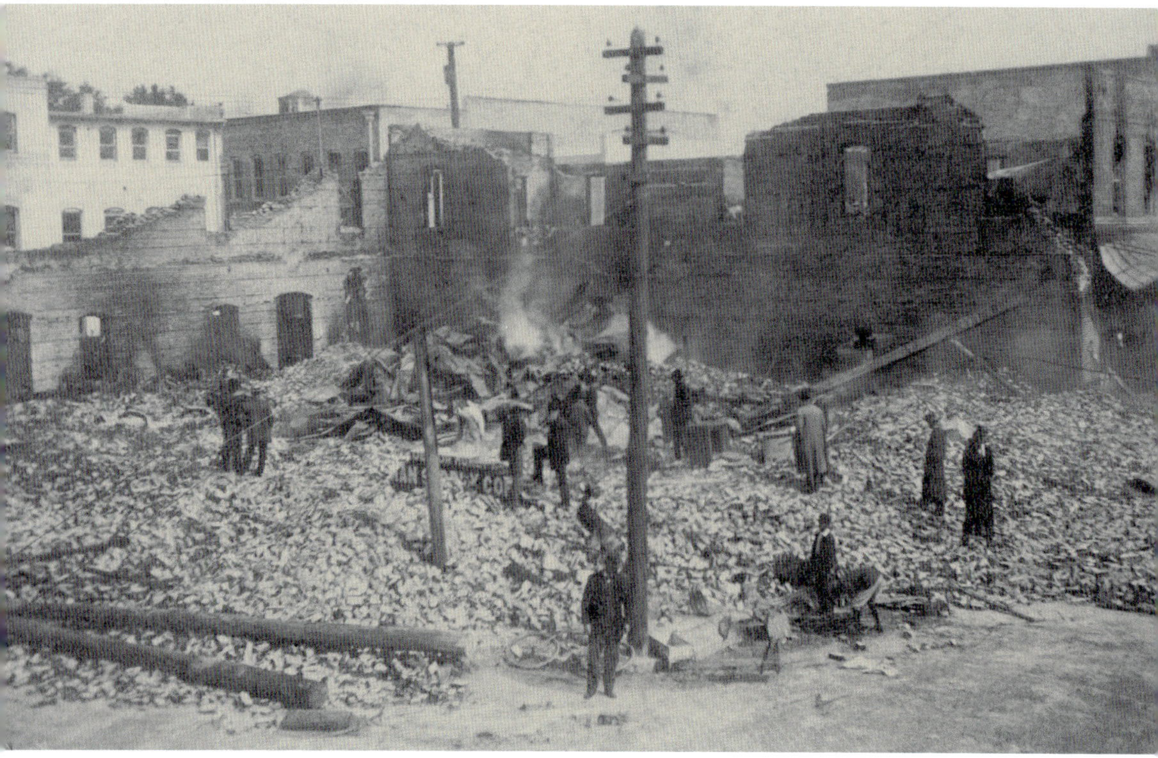

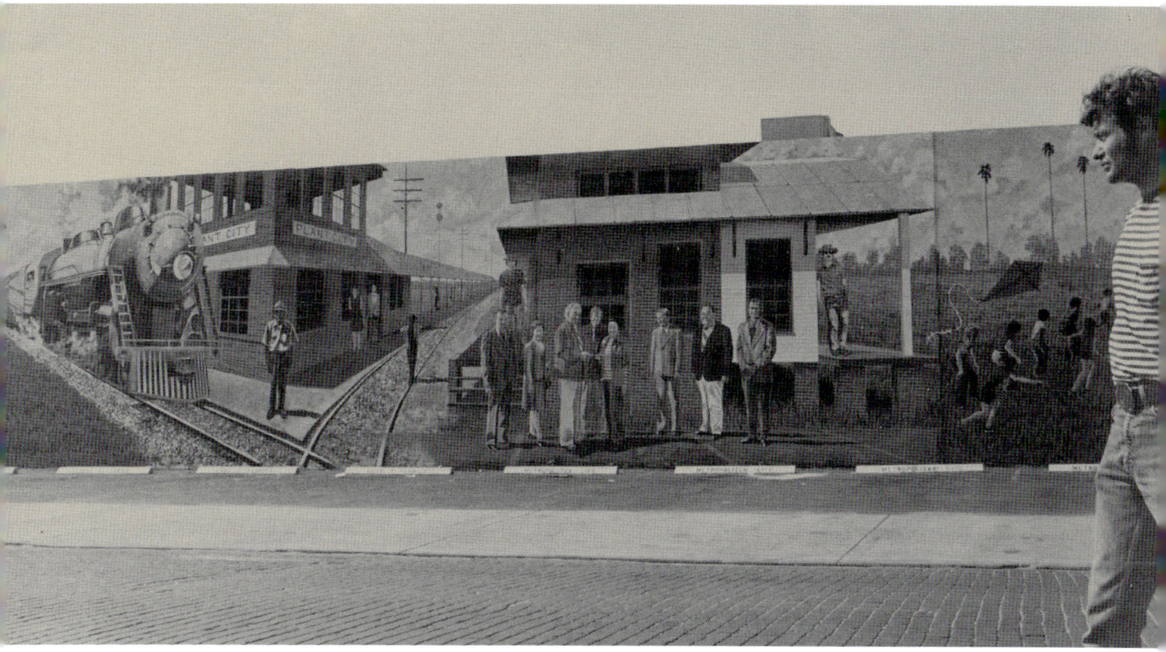

The Arts Council of Plant City, Fine Arts Council of Florida, and the National Endowment for the Arts (NEA) sponsored this 76-foot-by-23-foot outdoor mural at Collins and Haines Streets, painted by artist John Briggs. A fire drastically damaged this image of historical downtown Plant City in February 2005. The building with the mural *Reflection of a Town* was destroyed, and all that remained was the exterior wall with the mural. The remaining wall came down. Recognizing the value of this mural to the community, in March 2010 the East Hillsborough Historical Society and the Florida Strawberry Festival® sponsored a canvas replication of the mural, which now hangs in the festival's expo hall. Pictured are, from left to right, Calvin Belcher, engineer; Albert "Dummy" Keys, a baggage handler at the depot who was born deaf and could not speak; Catherine Fletcher Clark; Roy Thacker; Marva Porter Berry; John Briggs, artist; William D. "Billy" Vernon; Betty Jo Vernon; Dwight Nifong; Roger Johnson, president of the Plant City Arts Council; Grace Harrell; Hilman Bowden; Mac Hooper; James L. "Jim" Redman; and Gary Cameron. The children on the playground include Jackie Wiggins Chutter (third from left) and other members of Mr. Cameron's Cork Elementary School class.

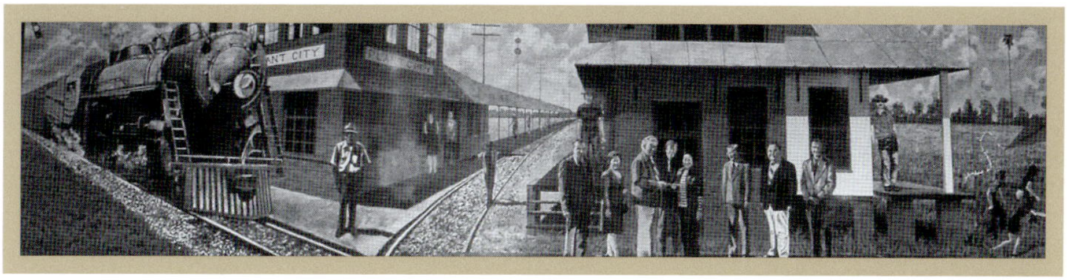

Plant City men have always served in the country's armed forces. Dr. W. E. Edwards served his community proudly as an officer in the Spanish-American War from 1898 to 1901. Chester R. Bender arrived with his family in Plant City from West Virginia in 1925. Upon graduation from Plant City High School, he became the first Floridian to graduate from the Coast Guard Academy in 1936. He was nominated by President Nixon on April 16, 1970, to be the commandant of the Coast Guard for a four-year term, with the four-star rank of admiral. Admiral Bender died in California on July 20, 1996, and was buried in Arlington National Cemetery will full military honors.

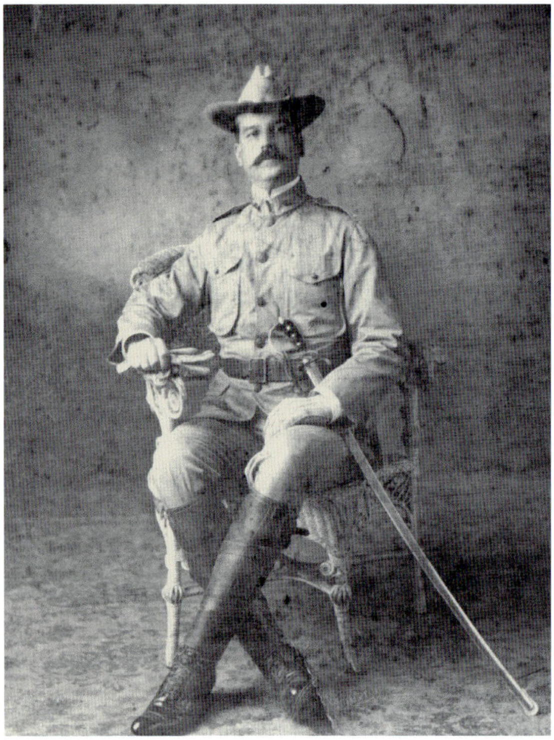

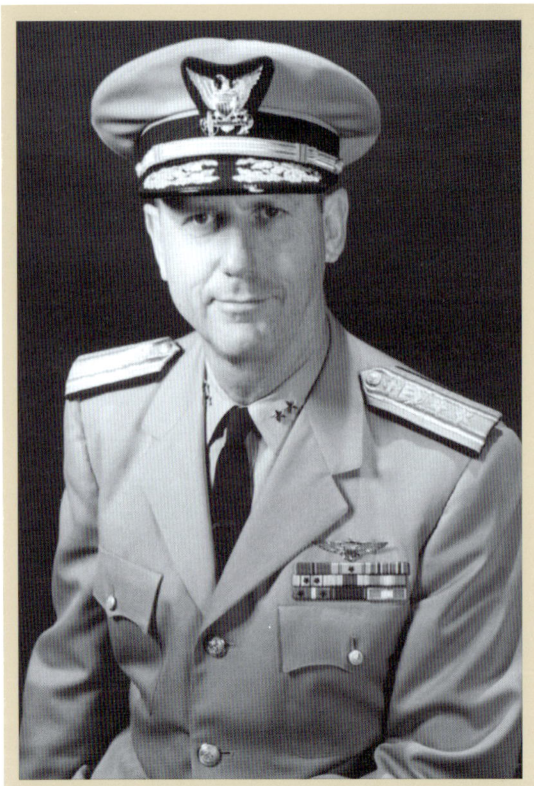

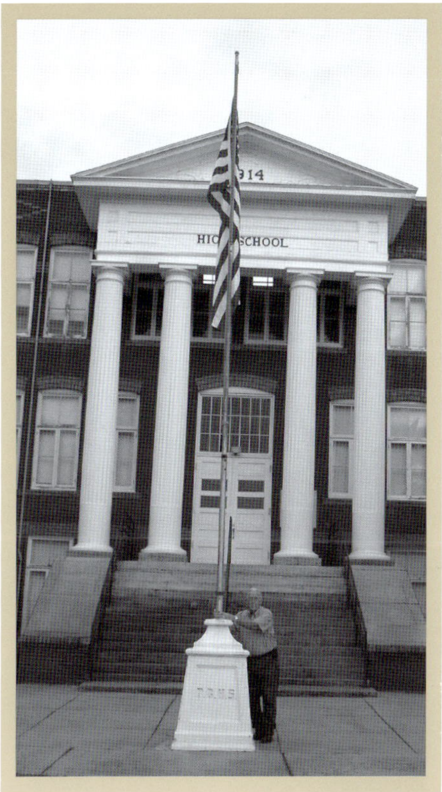

Answering the call to serve his country, on March 16, 1945, Royal Wise enlisted in the U.S. Army and reported for duty. He was stationed at Taegu, Korea, as a member of Canon Company First Battalion 6th Infantry Division. After his years of service, he returned to his hometown of Plant City, where he still resides. He continues to show his patriotism as he installs a new flag at the 1914 PCHSCC.

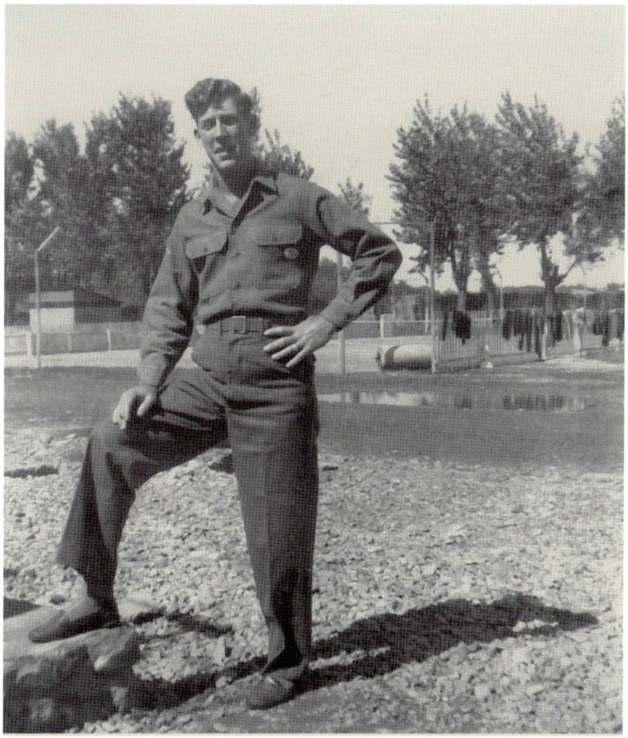

Community education was the goal for the Army National Guard's unit in attendance with a display of artillery and equipment at the local Pioneer Day in the 1980s. In the center of the August 2010 photograph at right is Plant City native U.S. Army captain Ryan Pless, 3rd Heavy Brigade Combat Team, 3rd Infantry Division at the Change of Command OIF VII in Iraq.

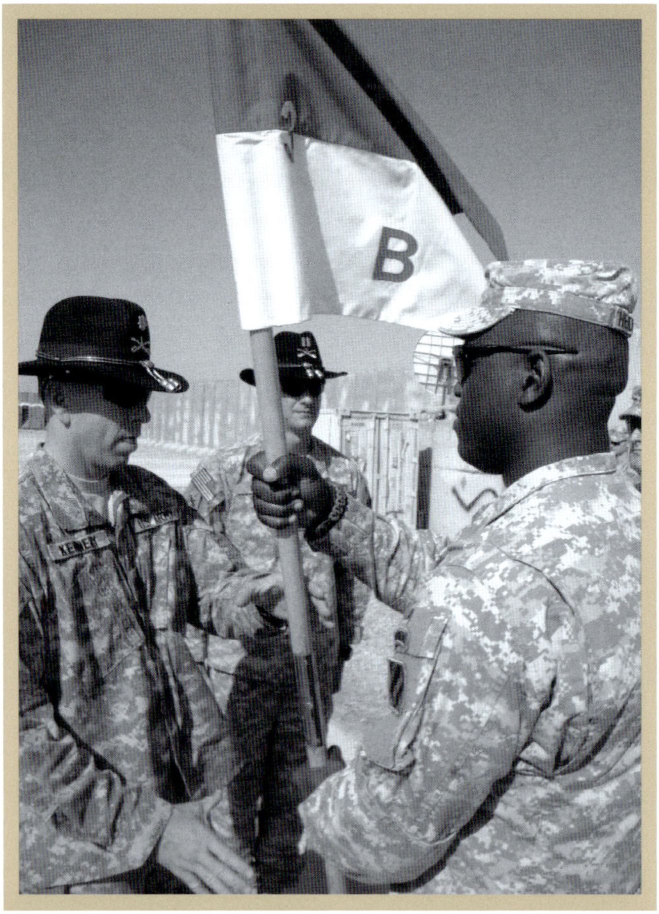

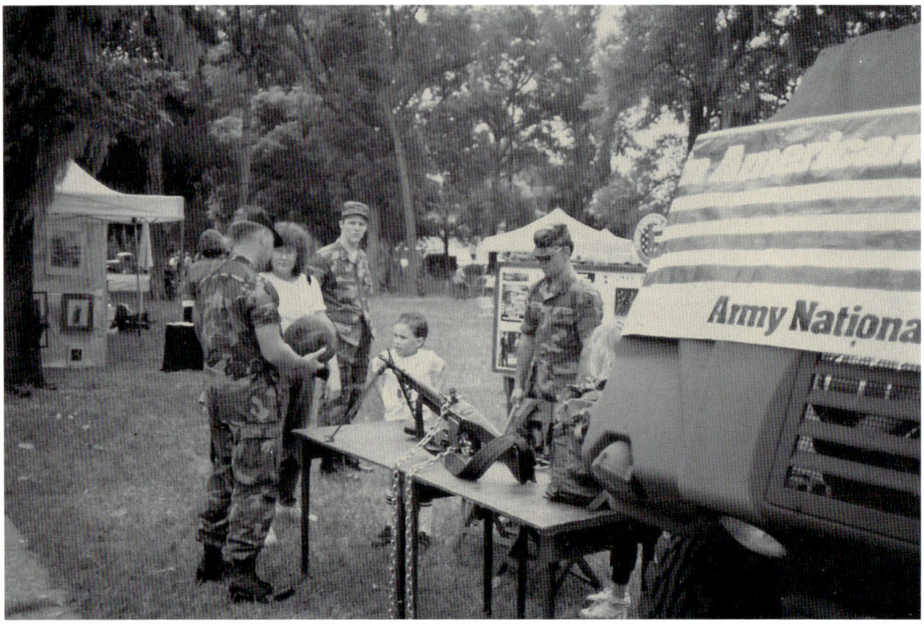

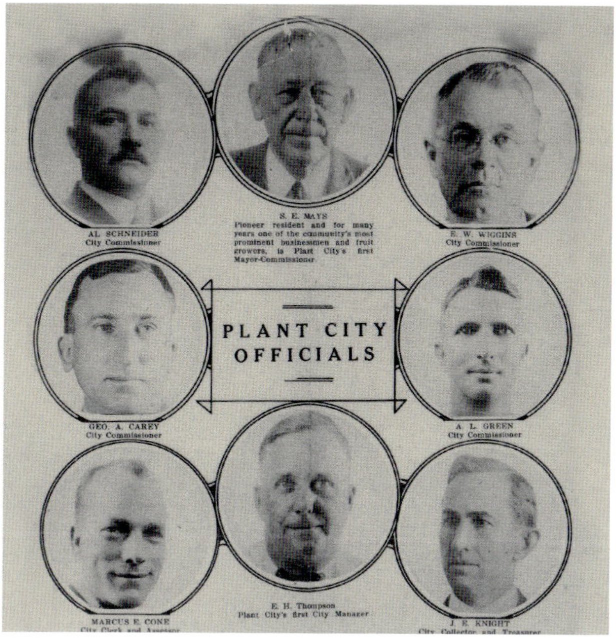

Early leadership of the town's prospering community was led by a group of local businessmen who were descendants of the early pioneers. They had come to Plant City with a desire to develop the community into one that they could be proud of. Pictured below after adjourning a recent city commission meeting, city officials at the time of publication are, from left to right, commissioners Michael S. Sparkman and Mary Yvette Thomas Mathis, city attorney Kenneth W. Buchman, Mayor Daniel D. Raulerson, city manager Gregory S. Horwedel, city clerk Kerri J. Miller, Vice Mayor William D. Dodson, and commissioner Rick A. Lott.

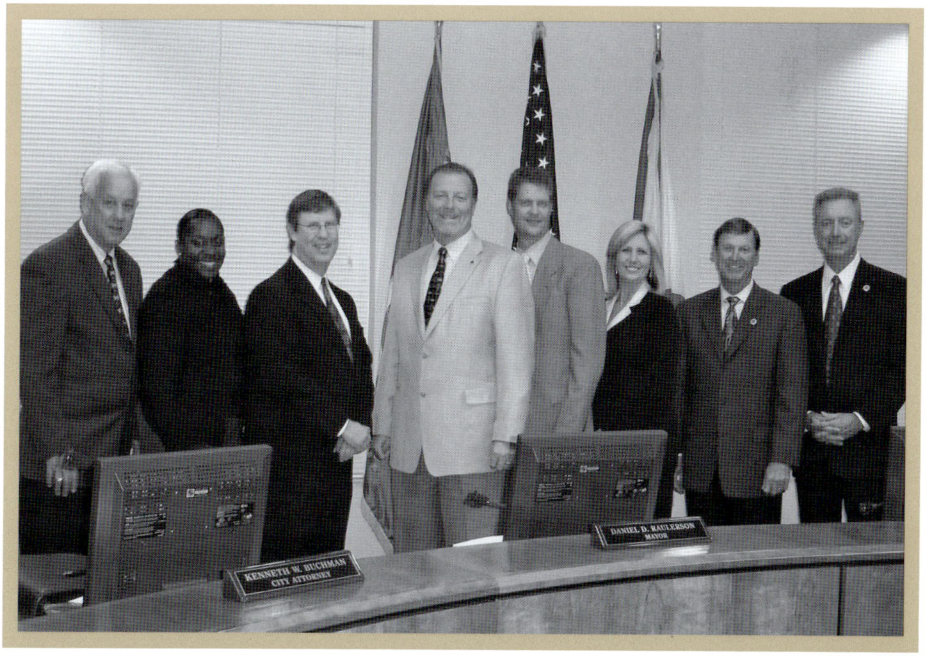

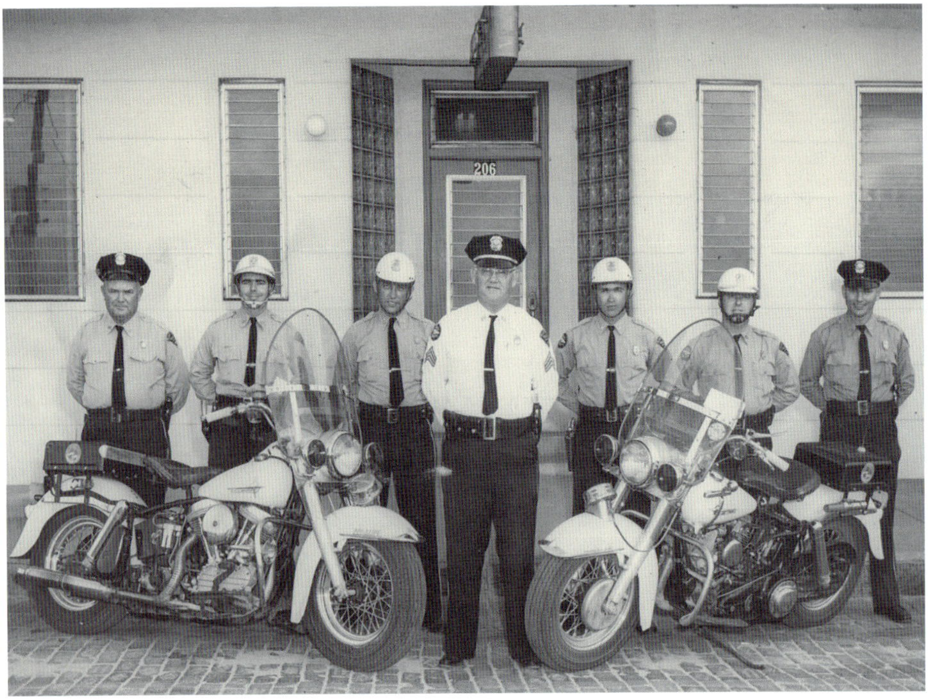

In the 1960s, the Plant City Police Department was located at 206 South Evers Street. Above is their seven-man unit of officers sworn to follow the law and provide protection for their community. Pictured from left to right are Roy Simmons, Bobby Helms, Donald Corley, Sgt. Seymour Sparkman, Gene Paul, Charles Crosby, and Ronald Haney. The department moved just a few blocks south on Collins Street in the former Publix Supermarket/Hillsborough Community College building. Needing to accommodate the ever-growing city, a new, much larger, state-of-the-art facility, the Michael S. Sparkman Police Center, was dedicated in 2007. In the 2010 photograph below are, from left to right, officers DeeDee Gregory and Russell Bass, chief of police William "Bill" McDaniel, and officers Fred "Tommy" Morris and Kyle Russell. The officers are members of the motor unit.

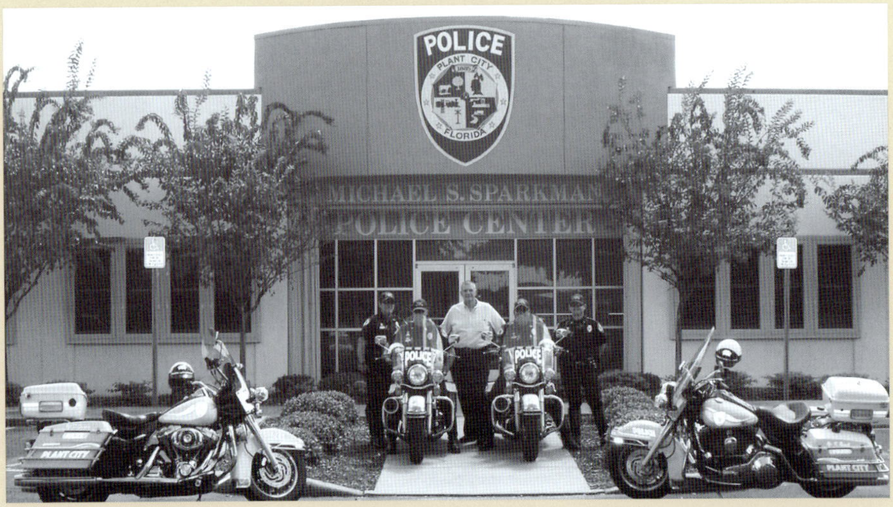

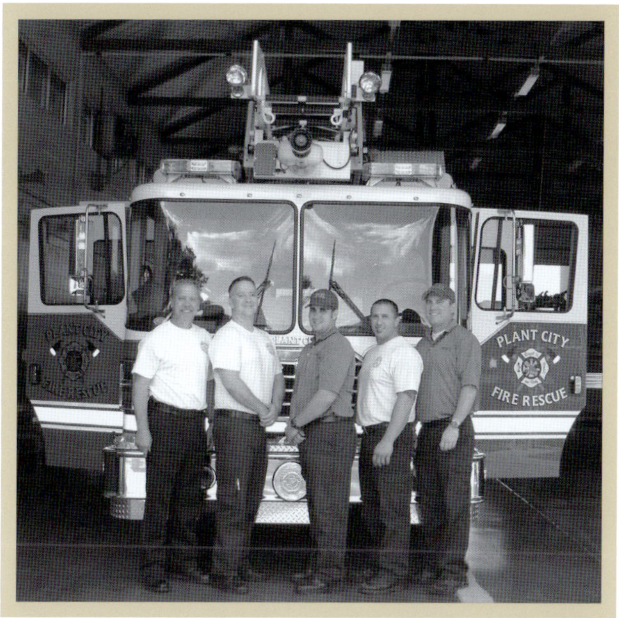

The 1923 city hall housed all the city offices, including the fire department. The first-floor location featured large bay doors to accommodate the fire trucks. The fire chief was ably assisted by his trusty "fire dog." Currently the city is serviced by two fire station locations with crews working 24-hour shifts for emergency response. Pictured from left to right are Capt. Nat Hargrove, firefighters Steve Gunnin, Billy Wimberly, and Lance Borges, and driver engineer David Jackson of Fire Station No. 1, located at 604 East Alexander Street.

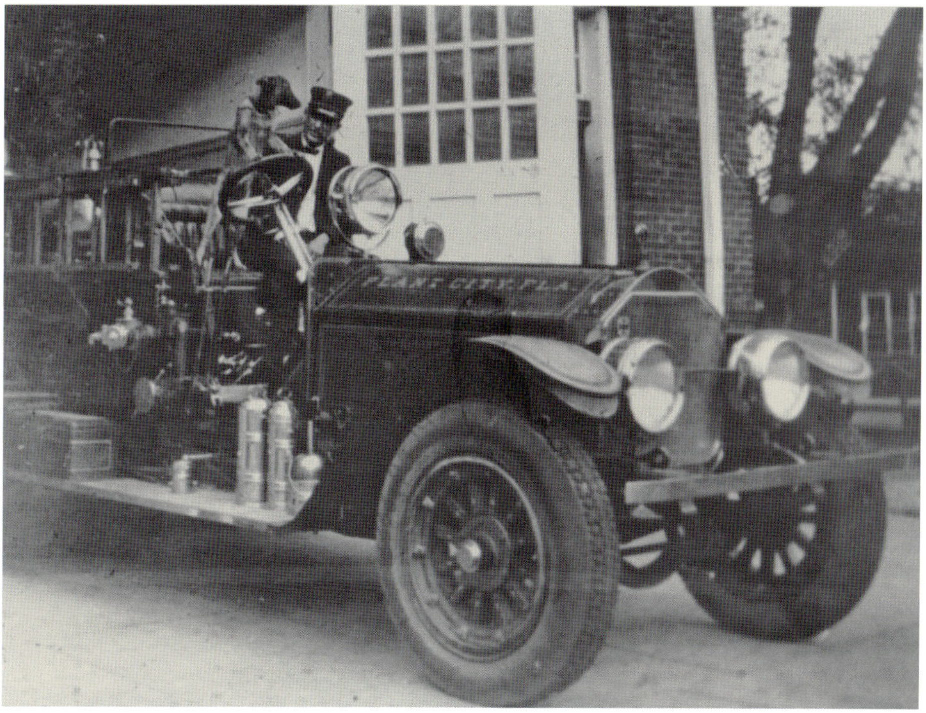

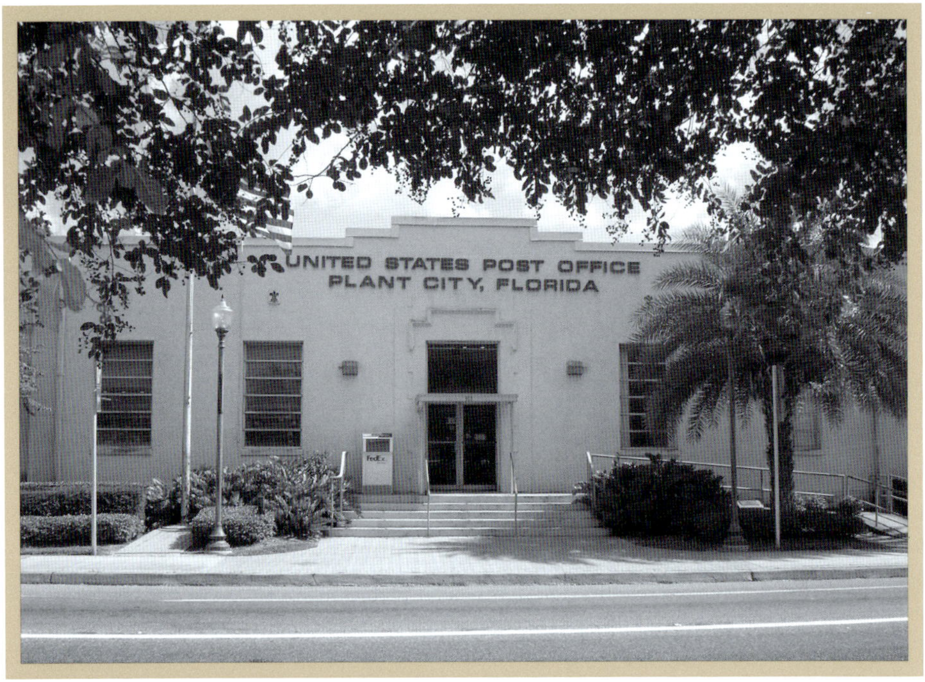

M. F. Tillman, the first rural mail carrier for Plant City, stands in front of the post office at the northeast corner of Reynolds and Collins Streets in 1903. The downtown post office, built in 1935, is located at the corner of Reynolds and Wheeler Streets. This location is currently on a list for closure, and Plant City would only be serviced by the facility located in the Walden Woods area, which is 2 miles from the downtown site.

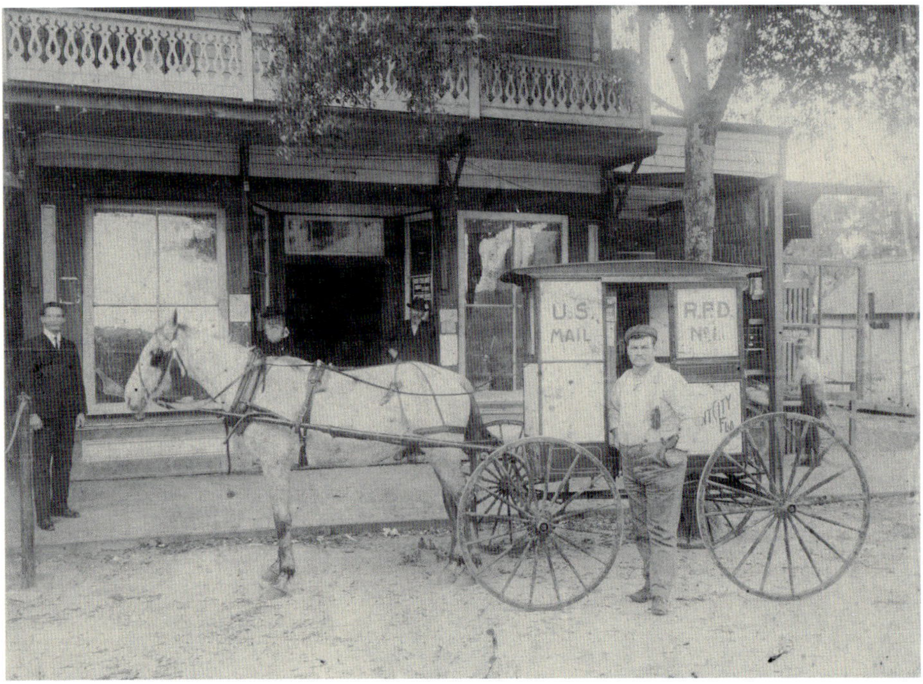

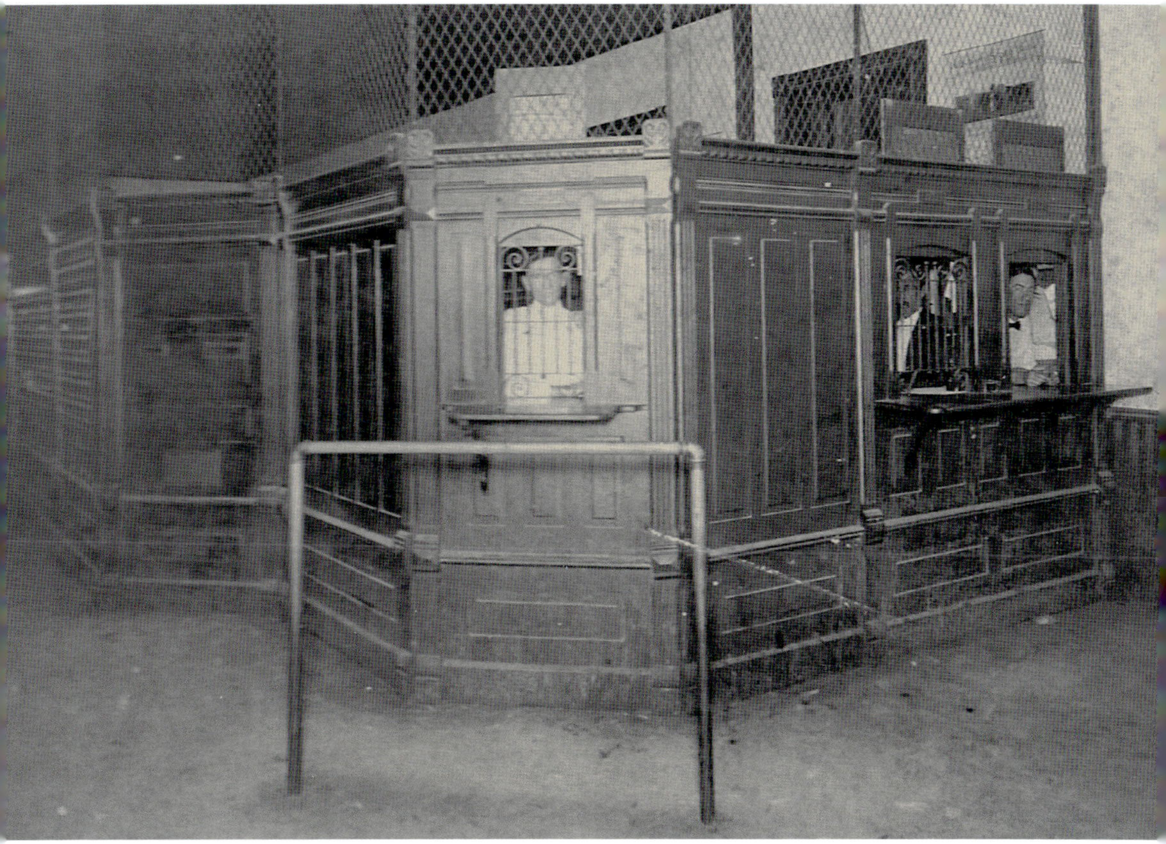

Sporting a black bow tie and shown on the far right, Charles Curtis Anderson was a mail clerk at the Plant City Post Office in 1915. Patsy, the post office clerk at the downtown Plant City Post Office, enjoys greeting customers. The facility still has postal boxes used by many of Plant City's businesses and residents. Mamie E. Barnes was the postmaster when the service first moved to this building in 1935. Automation and technology have vastly evolved since Barnes's days as postmaster.

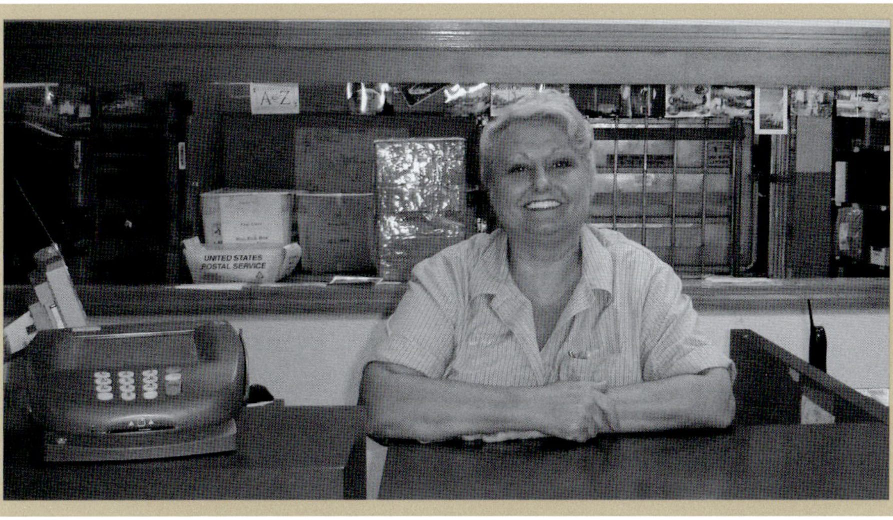

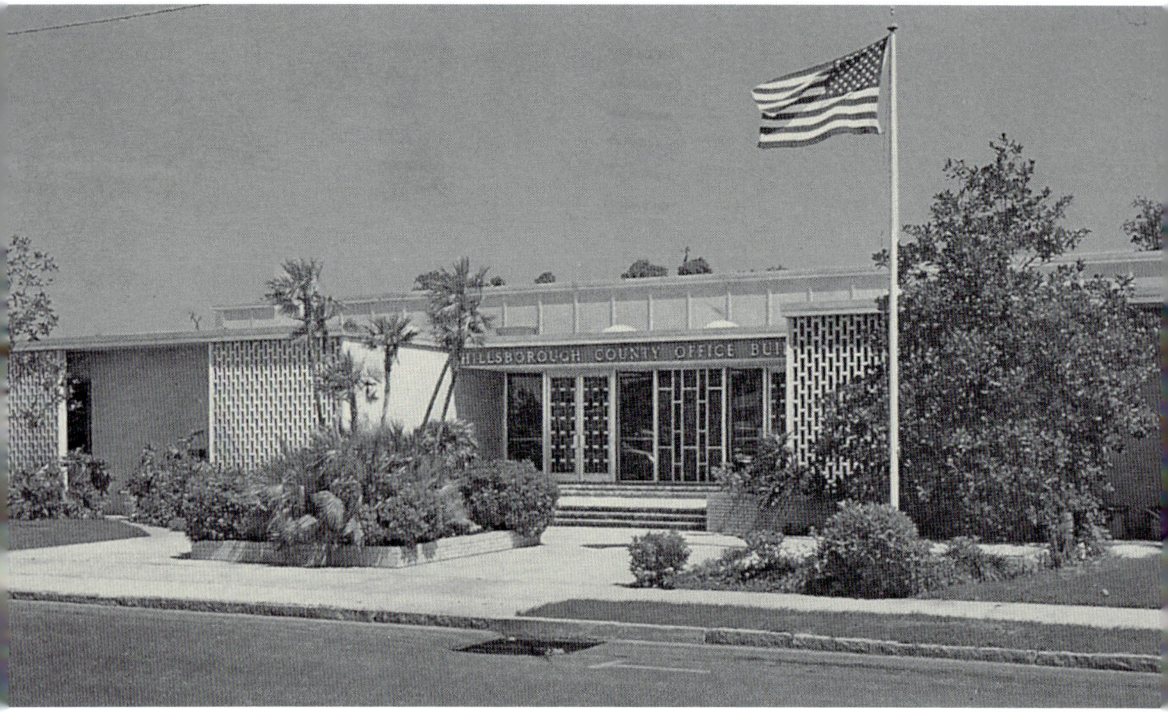

Residents of the eastern Hillsborough County area could transact their county government services in the Hillsborough County office building located between Reynolds and Baker Streets along Michigan Avenue. Clerk of the courts, licensing, property, and health department divisions provided services that previously required traveling to Tampa. At the time of publication, construction crews have started working on a new 60,000-square-foot building, and the old structure will be demolished for parking. The site of the expansion was the location of some of Plant City's early automobile dealerships.

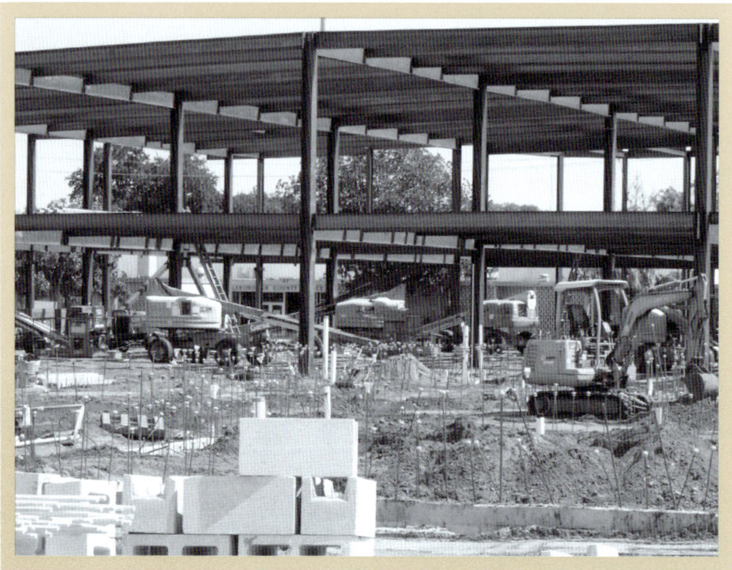

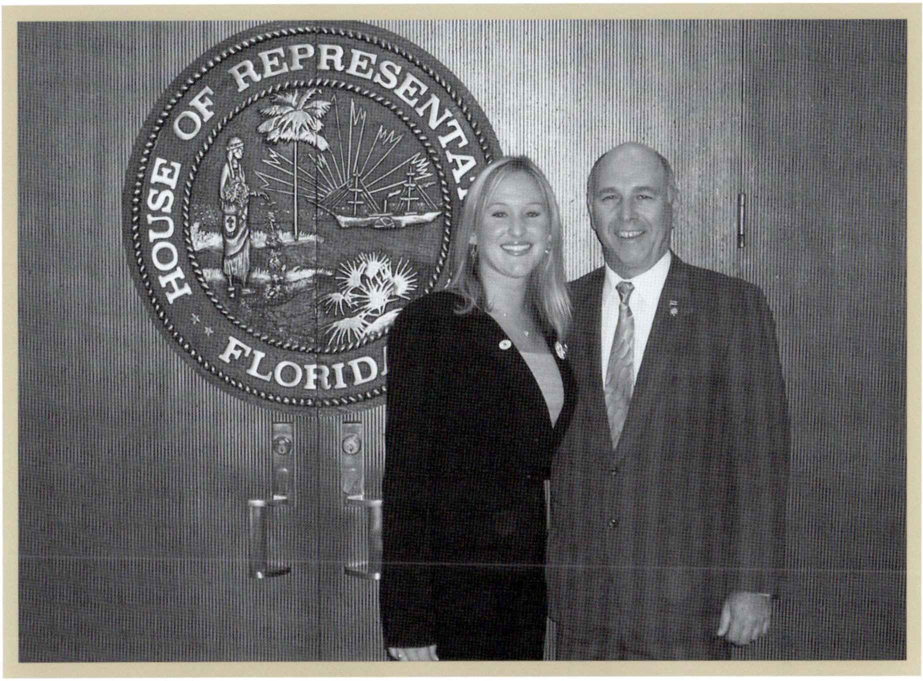

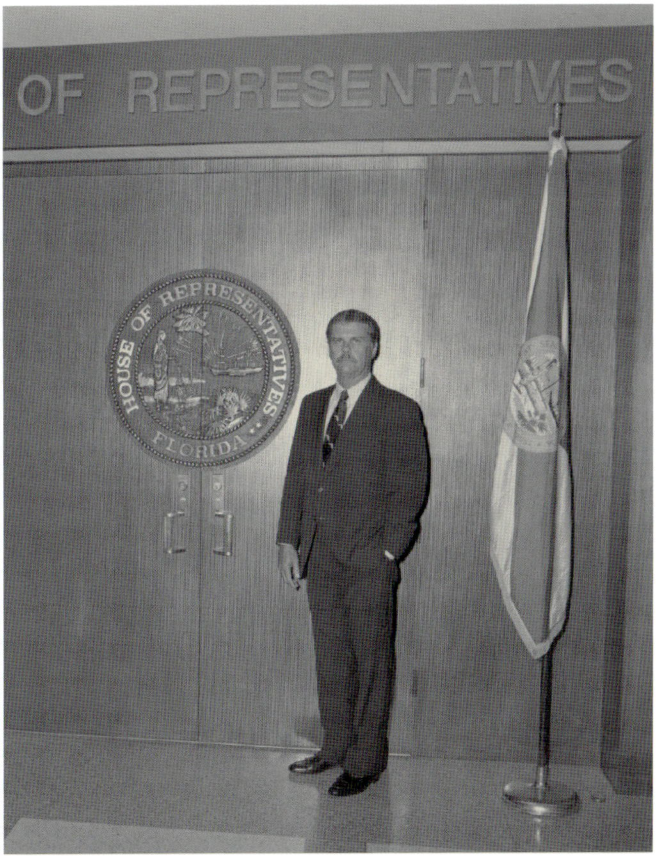

Plant City has been represented in state government offices for more than the last century. Elected to the Florida House of Representatives in 1978, Carl Carpenter had also served on the Hillsborough County Commission and the School Board of Hillsborough County. He is a graduate of the University of Florida School of Pharmacy. Currently representing the district is Richard "Rich" Glorioso, former City of Plant City commissioner and retired U.S. Air Force colonel, who spent 27 years in the military.

Longtime local lore stated that the two water towers were for hot and cold water; the larger Plant City tower provided locals with fresh cold water. Downtown properties were served by the public water works, thus eliminating the need for a picture pump on the back porch. As the city limits expanded and the town's population grew, additional water towers were erected on the east, south, and west sides of the community. The east side tank is painted like a strawberry, the fruit that put Plant City on the map.

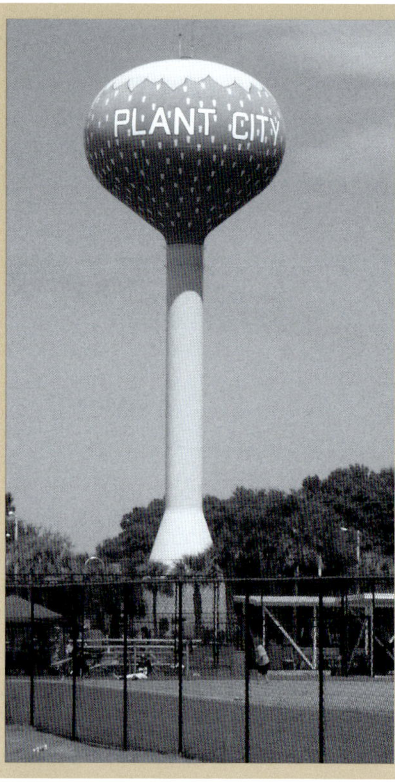

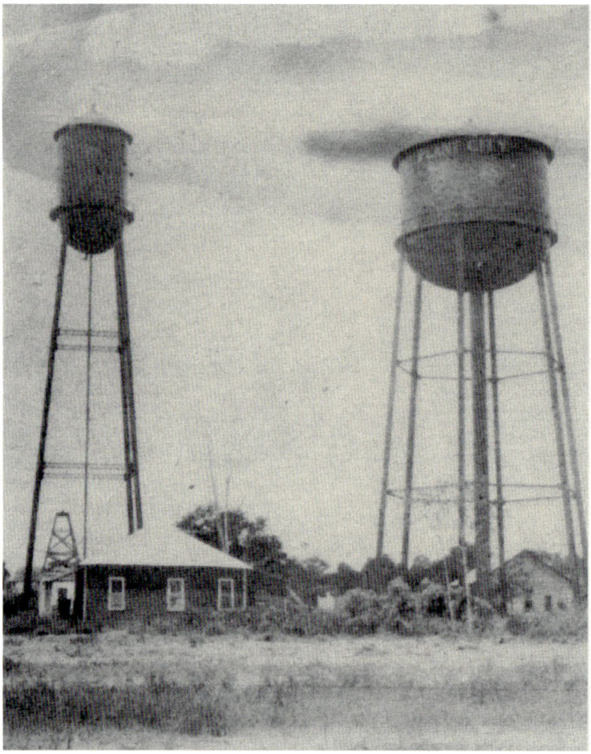

CHAPTER 2

BUSINESS

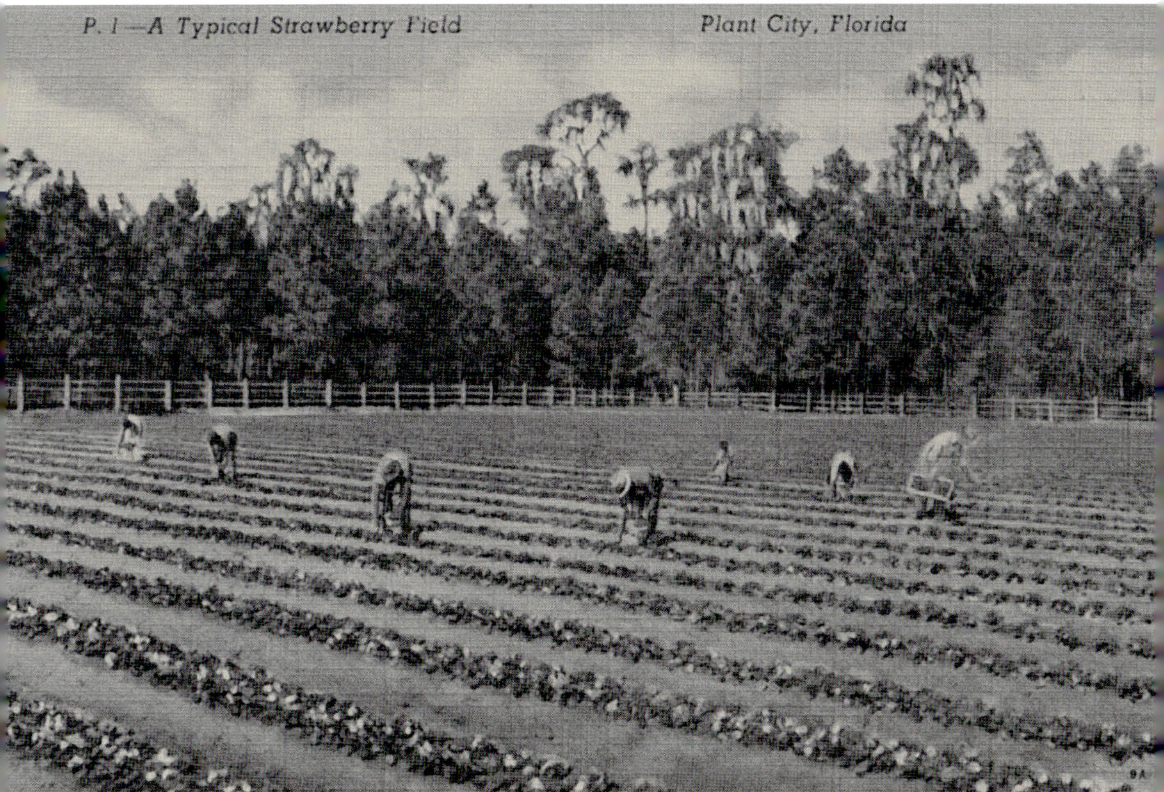

Plant City has been well known for the businesses that focused on the agricultural industry. Strawberries, citrus fruit, and truck farm vegetables were the cash crops that supported this community. Planting and harvesting methods have evolved through the years, including the elimination of the "strawberry school" schedule, which planned the student school year calendar around the harvesting of the berry. The phosphate industry also was an early major contributor to the wealth of this community.

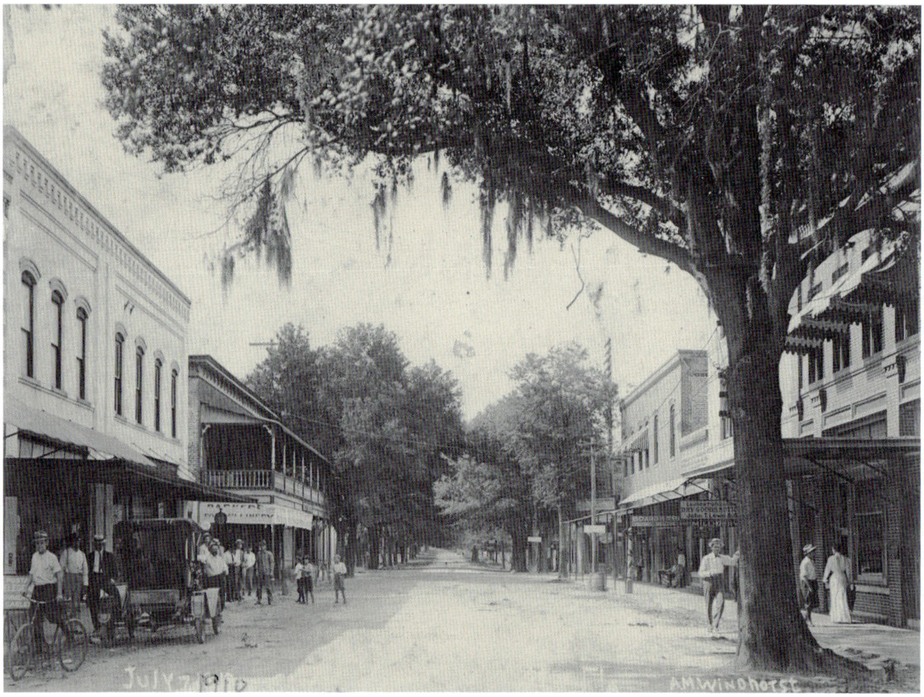

Collins Street has always been the heart of downtown. The 1910 image by photographer A. M. Windhorst shows newly built multistory brick buildings with storefronts to serve all the needs of the locals. Men conducted their business at the Plant City Board of Trade, while ladies shopped for the finest and latest fashions at the Barkers Millinery or John T. Lowe and Company Dry Goods. Shopping centers and malls have changed the use of the downtown buildings, yet their historical character is maintained through the local historic district designation. The Downtown Commercial Historic District is listed on the local and national registers.

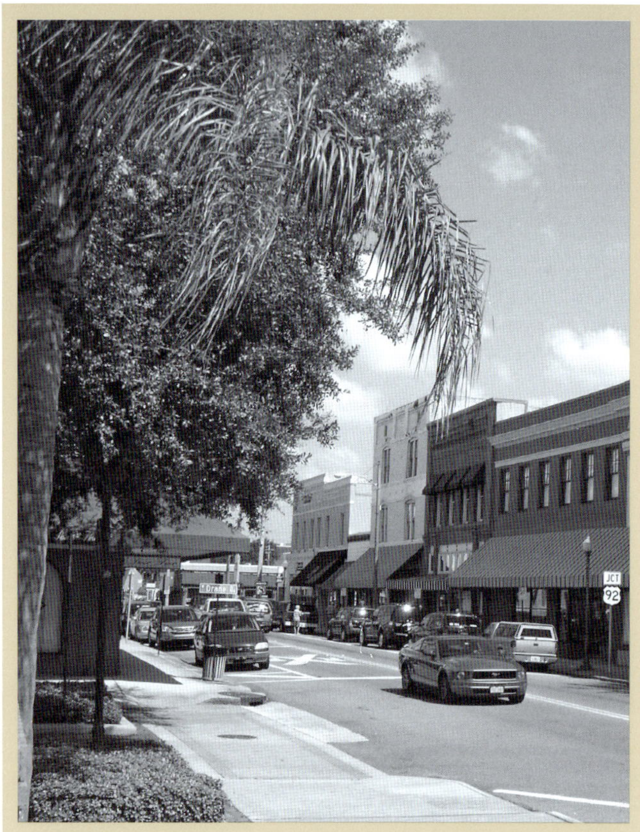

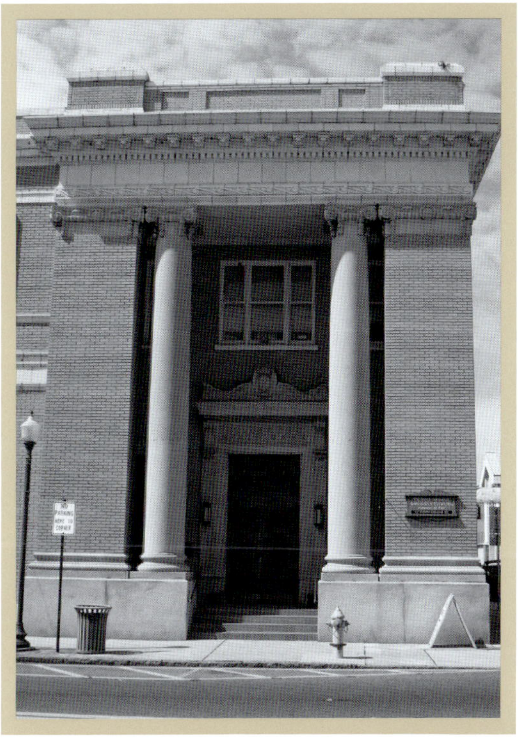

Plant City is in the central area of Florida. The downtown directional lamppost pointed north to Crystal Springs, south to Coronet, east to Lakeland, and west to Tampa. The early photograph of the Hillsboro State Bank building, constructed in 1914 of yellow brick with terra-cotta detailing is of the Beaux-Arts style. A wise owl stands guard over the double-door entrance to the offices of Trinkle, Redman, Swanson and Coton, P.A., attorneys at law. The building is individually listed on the National Register of Historic Sites.

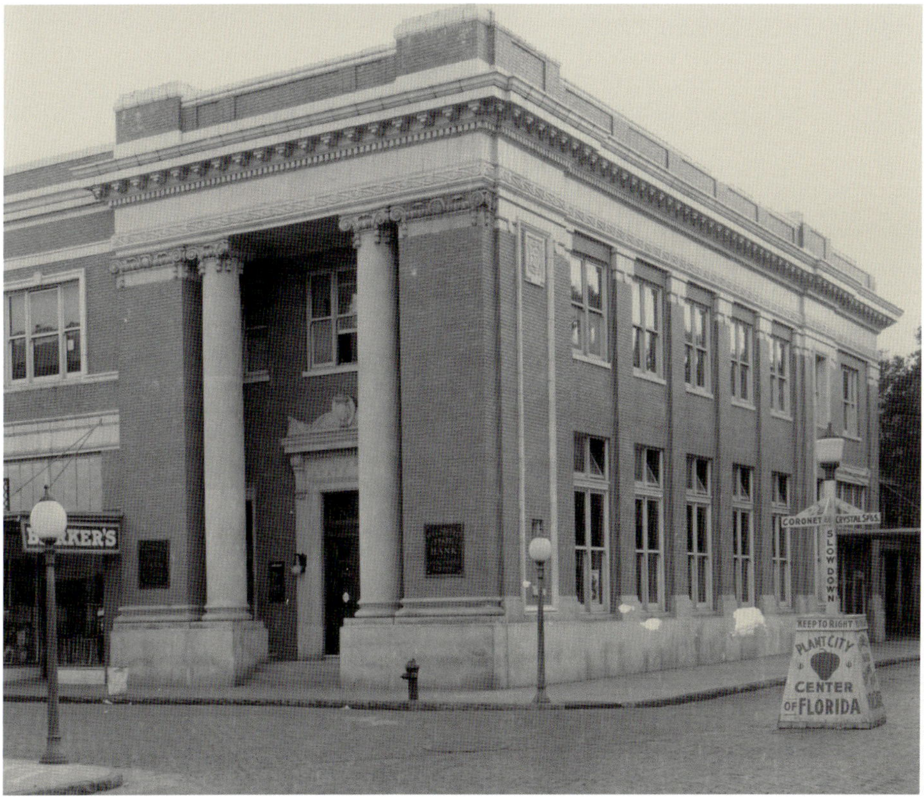

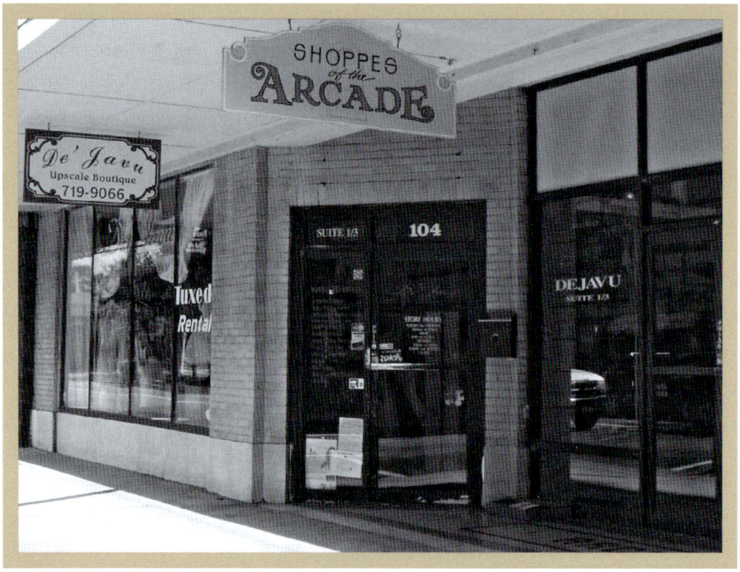

Local contractors Dudley and Nulter constructed the Arcade building in 1925 for the heirs of the Wright family at a cost of $50,000. Formed in 1954, First Federal Savings and Loan Association had their offices on the Reynolds Street facade. The Reynolds Street location has been occupied by optometrists and restaurants and is now the site of De' Javu, an upscale boutique offering tuxedo rentals for social occasions.

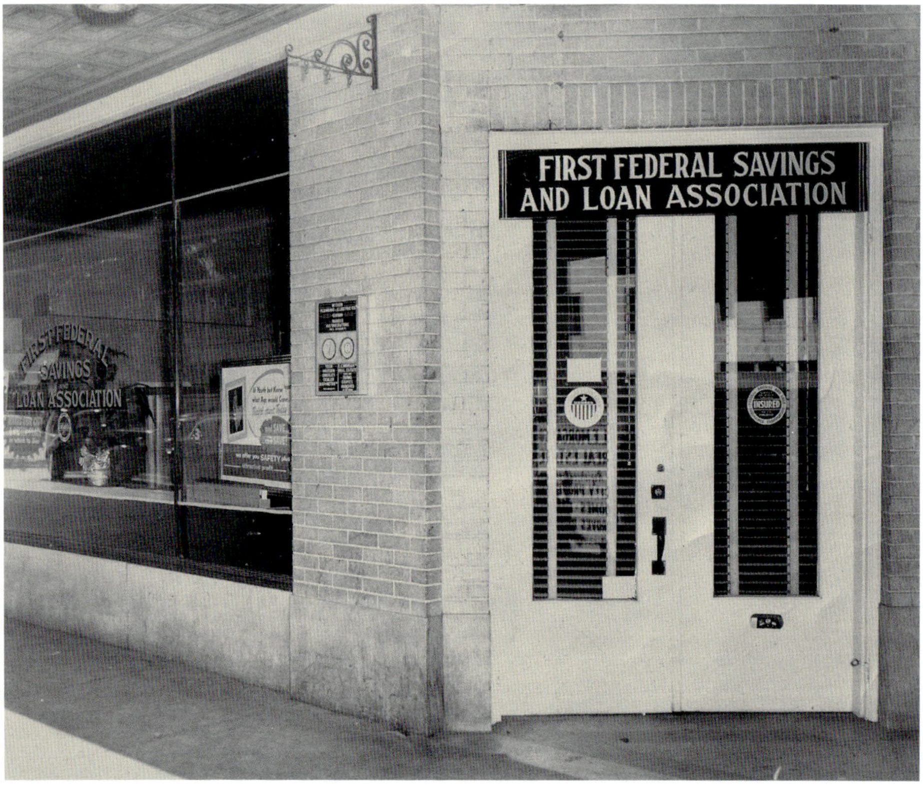

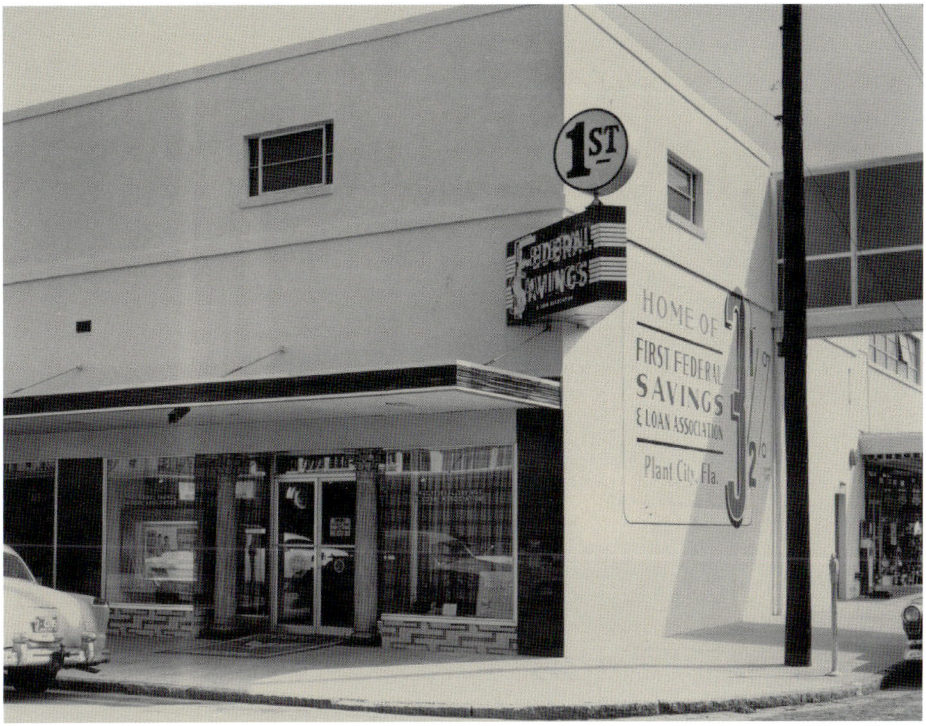

In 1957, First Federal Savings and Loan Association moved across the street to the northwest side of the McCrory Building. It advertised 3.5 percent interest rates in 1958. The enclosed walkway seen above the street was connected to the Hillsboro State Bank building and its drive-in facility located on the southwest corner of Evers and Reynolds Streets. The growth of First Federal allowed for its purchase of property in 1960 and the construction of the current facility. The name was changed to Sunshine State Federal Savings and Loan Association in 1975.

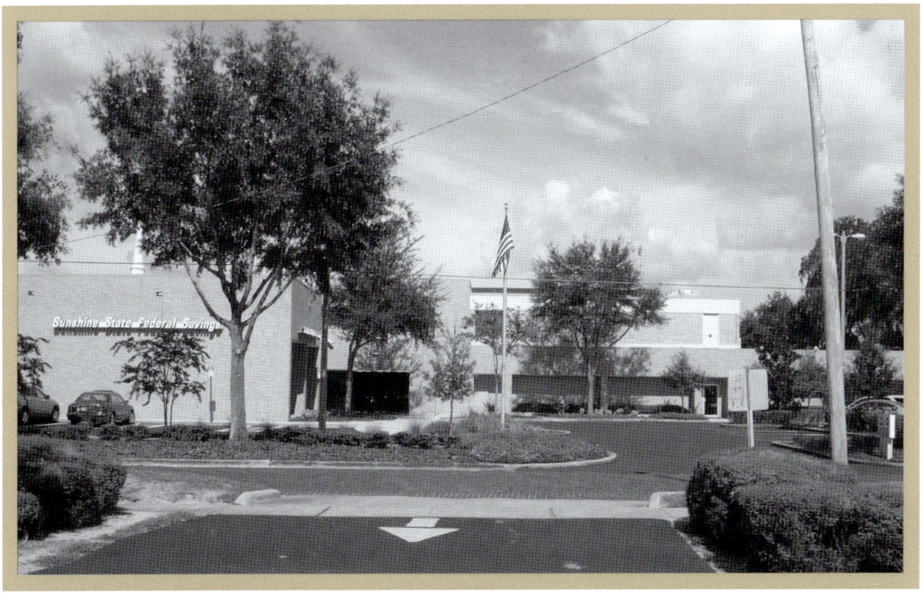

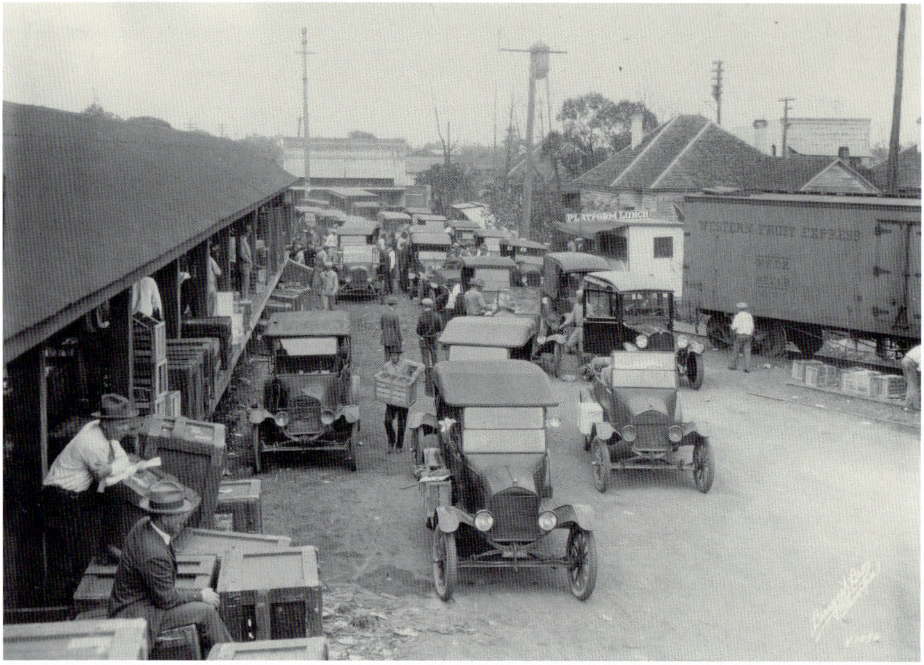

In the early 1920s, the local farmers brought their vegetables, packed in hampers or crates, to the local market for selling and loading straight onto the Seaboard Lines rail cars on East Reynolds Street. Bidding, buying, and shipping of strawberries took place here at the Berry Yard. Seaboard Lines constructed a new freight depot in 1946, and as seen in the current photograph, it is now the local station for the CSX rail track crew.

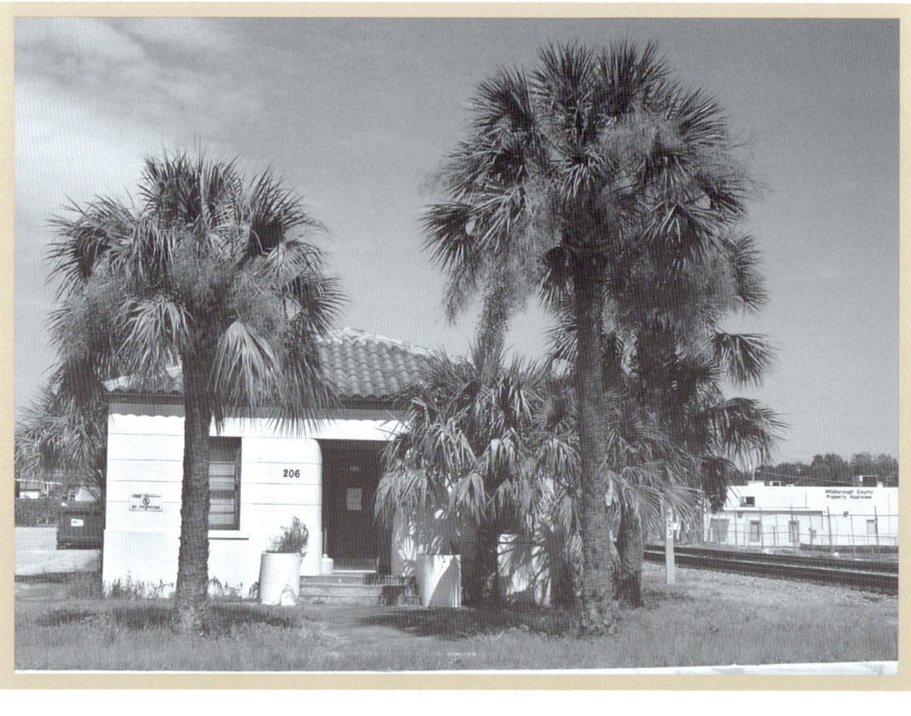

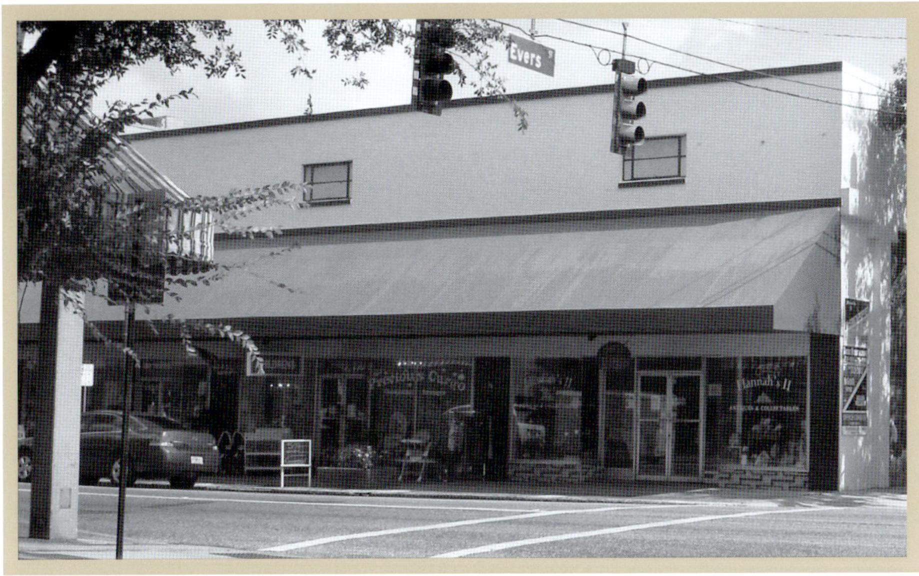

The Colonial Hotel, as seen below in this early 1920s postcard, had the second story added three years after its construction in 1910. Built on the former site of a livery business at a cost of $15,000, the hotel closed its doors in 1926. The property was purchased by J. G. McCrory for expansion of his Collins Street dime store. The Reynolds and Collins Streets storefronts are now occupied by antiques and clothing shops. The Evers Street location is home to the Greater Plant City Chamber of Commerce.

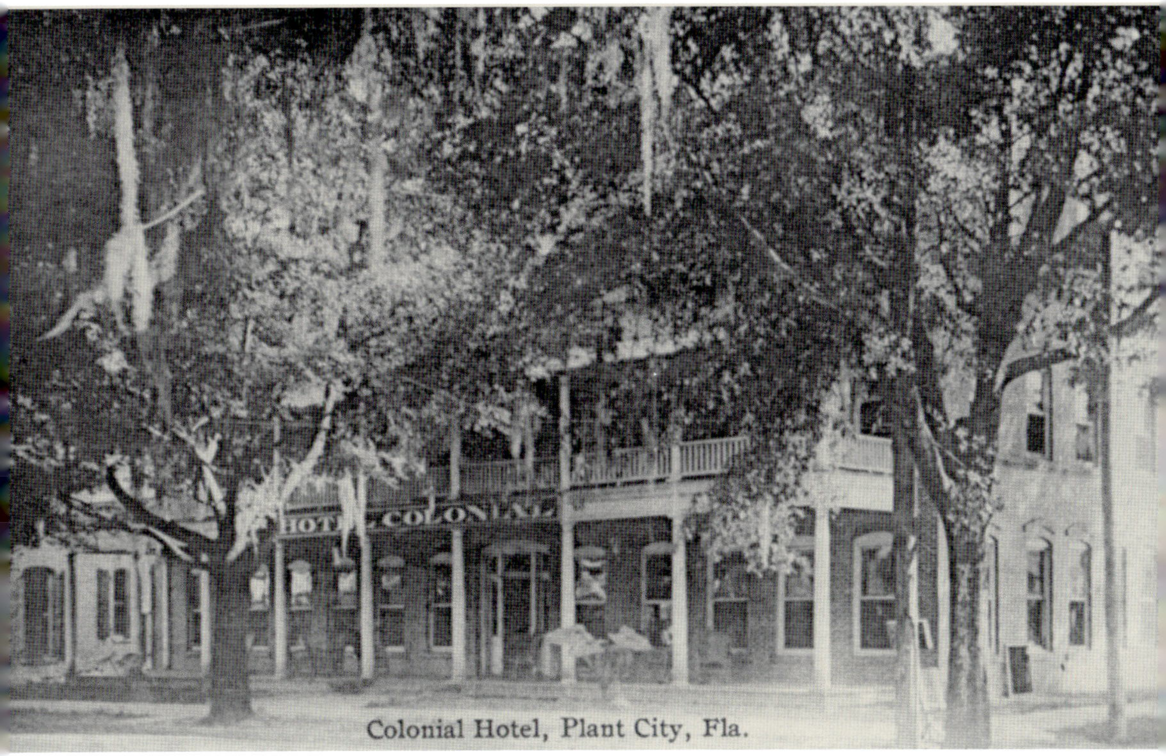

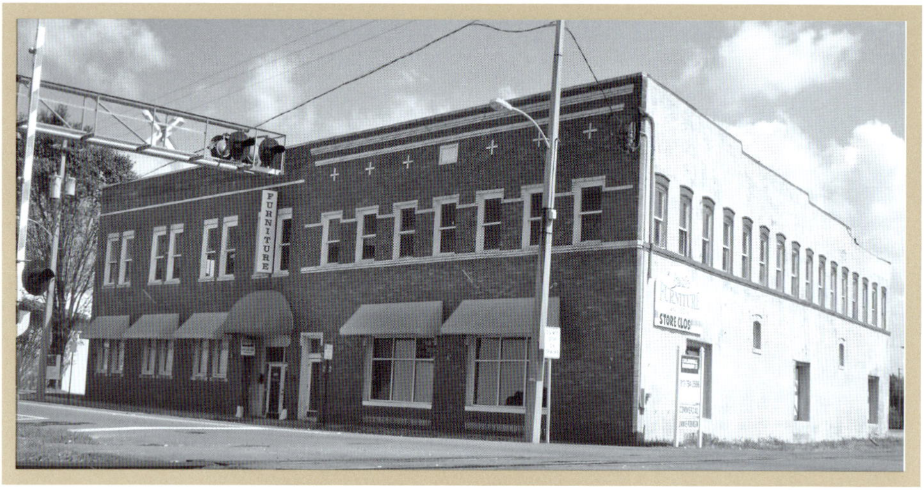

The Kilgore Seed Company constructed this two-story brick building at the Seaboard Lines tracks on South Collins Street in 1916. The building was 50 feet wide by 103 feet deep and cost a total of $7,000. Rail-side loading bays allowed for the easy loading and unloading of the seeds. The seed business was started by Flossie Motes Kilgore, and recognizing its success, her husband, Madison Kilgore, gave up his barbershop business and joined her. The building, as shown in the current photograph, still maintains its open floor plan and has recently housed a furniture store.

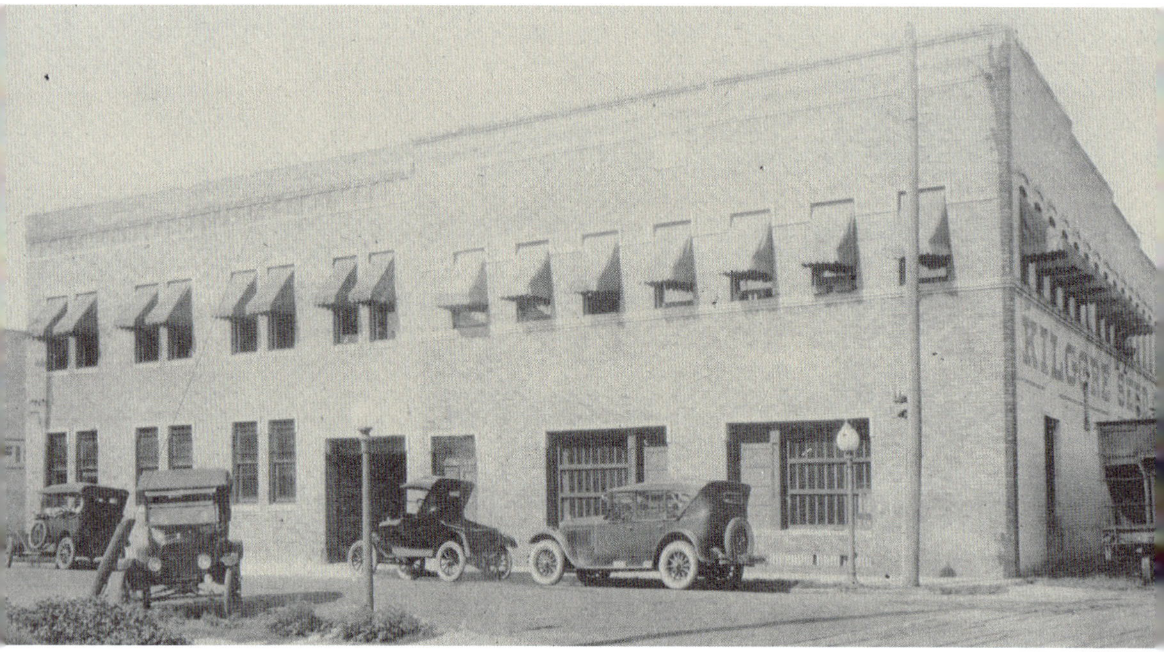

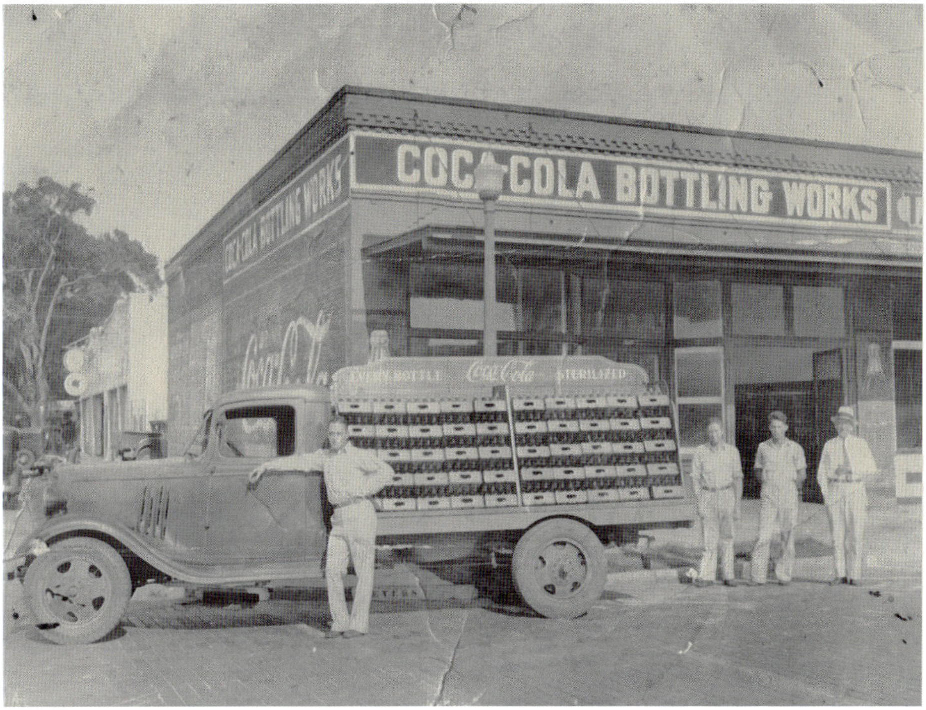

One of the fastest growing concerns in Plant City in 1927 was the Coca-Cola Bottling Works. J. W. Henderson, proprietor and manager, delivered his product in a mule-drawn wagon. In this early 1930s photograph of their new delivery truck are, from left to right, Ray Lominac, Jesse Wright, Wallace Wilson, and J. W. Henderson. This building, constructed by S. E. Mays in 1910, is now the location of the B & B Factory, a bedding and household furniture store.

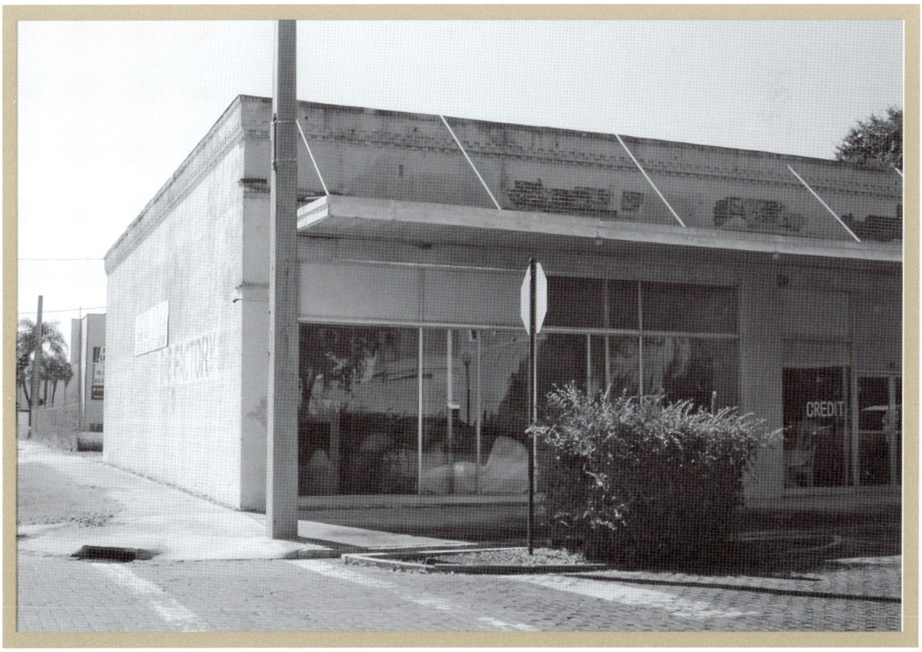

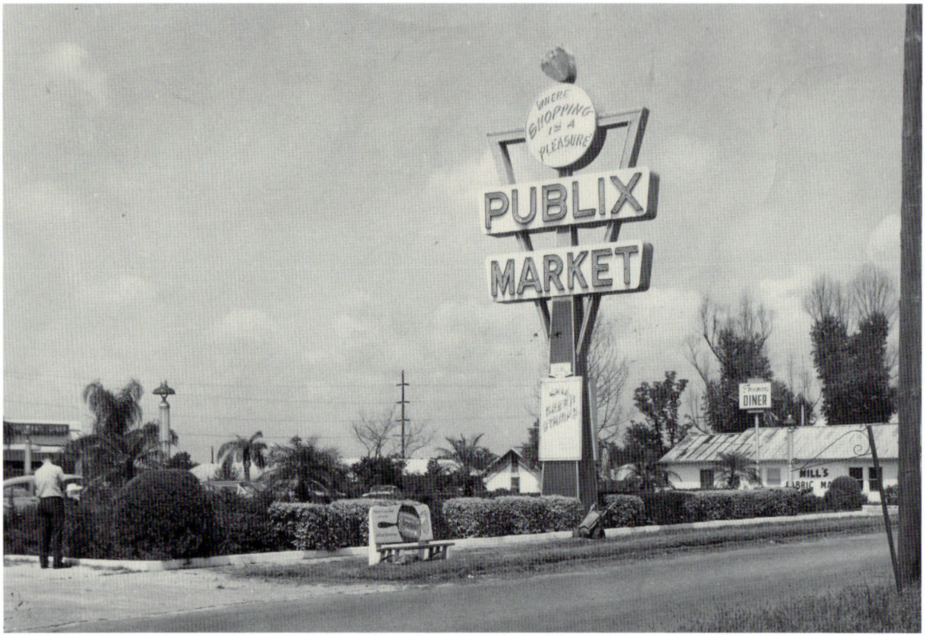

This 1960s South Collins Street location was the third site of the city's Publix Market. The longtime slogan, "Where Shopping is a Pleasure," and the distribution of S & H Green Stamps trading coupons made this a very popular grocery store. The building was later converted to the city's first campus for Hillsborough Community College, then police headquarters, and now is a vacant site awaiting the redevelopment of Plant City's midtown area. The adjacent mill's fabric mart building is now the Gold and Jewelry store and has historical theme scenes painted on both the north and south facades.

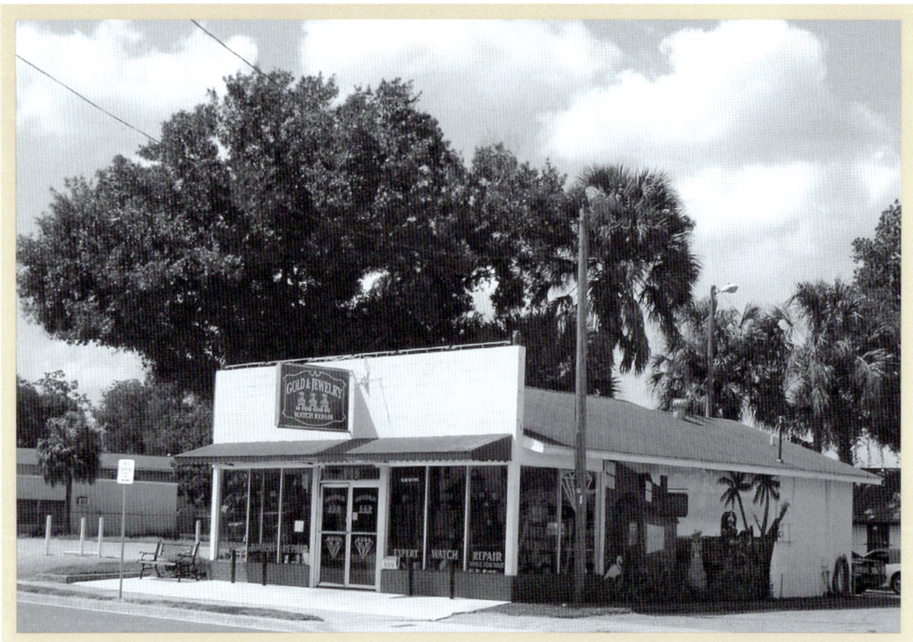

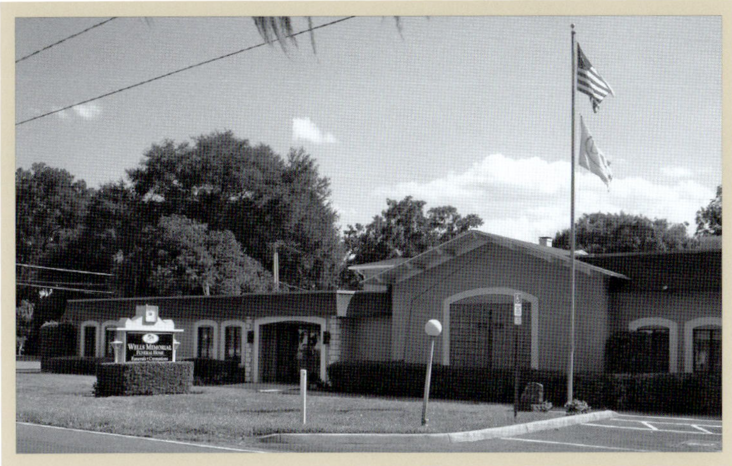

The Knights-Wordehoff home, located at the corner of Reynolds and Wheeler Streets, was moved in 1928 to the backside of the block fronting Mahoney Street and became the Wells Funeral Home in 1935. The early 1970s photograph of the building was taken before it was demolished in 1975 for expansion of city hall. During this time, other local funeral homes were consolidated and the Wells Memorial Funeral Home is shown in its current location at 1903 West Reynolds Street.

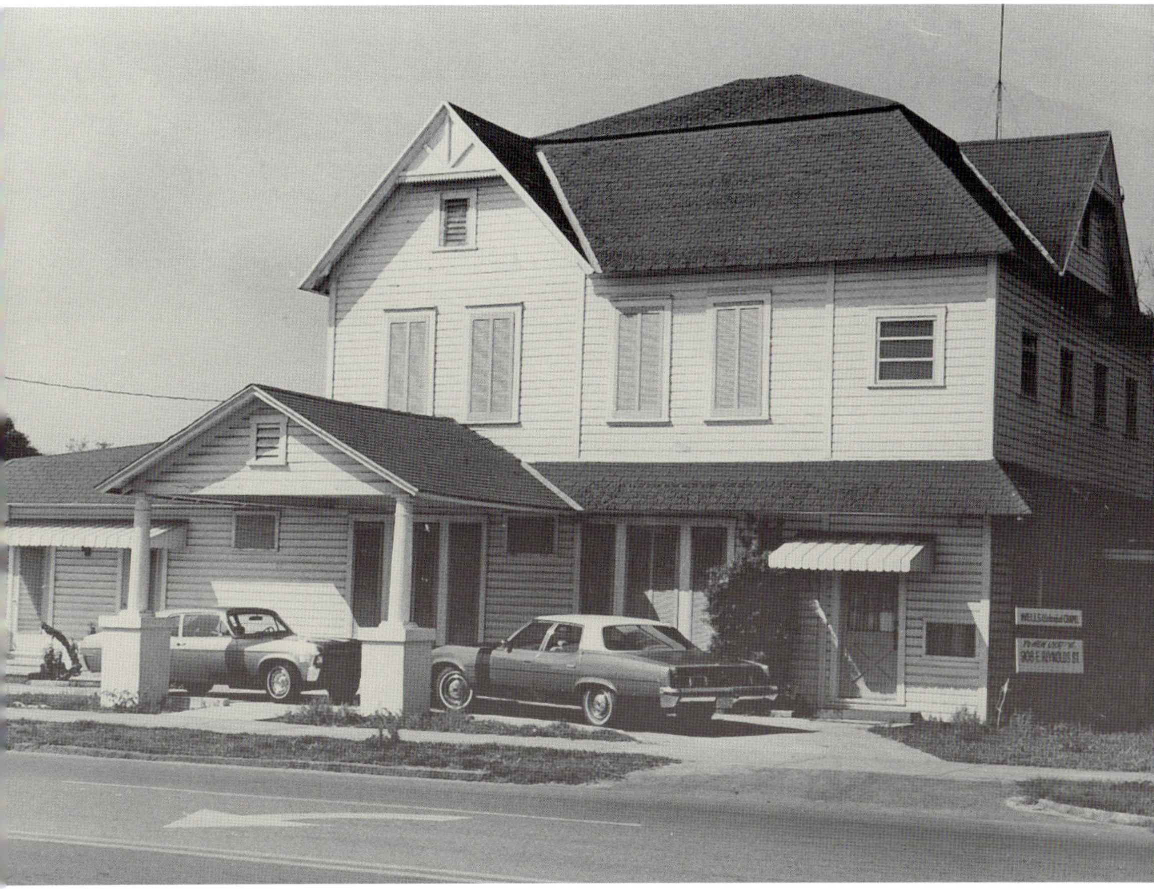

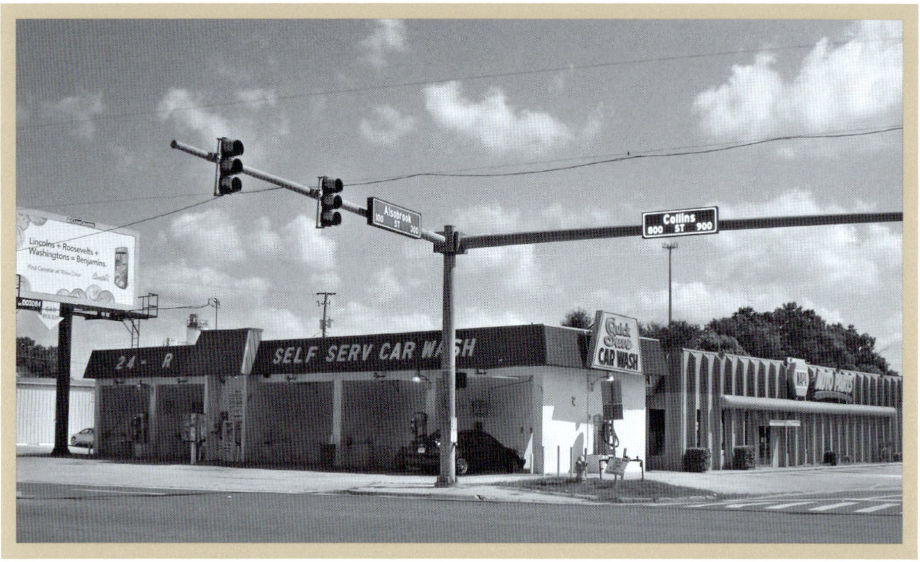

When the automobile came to town, so did the service station. The northeast corner of Collins and Alsobrook Streets was the site of the Standard Oil Company station, which offered full service for its customers in the first part of the 20th century. By the end of this era, the site had become the location for a self-serve car wash and the new Napa Auto Parts store, as seen in the current photograph. One of Plant City's business intersections, the brick streets have long been paved over with asphalt.

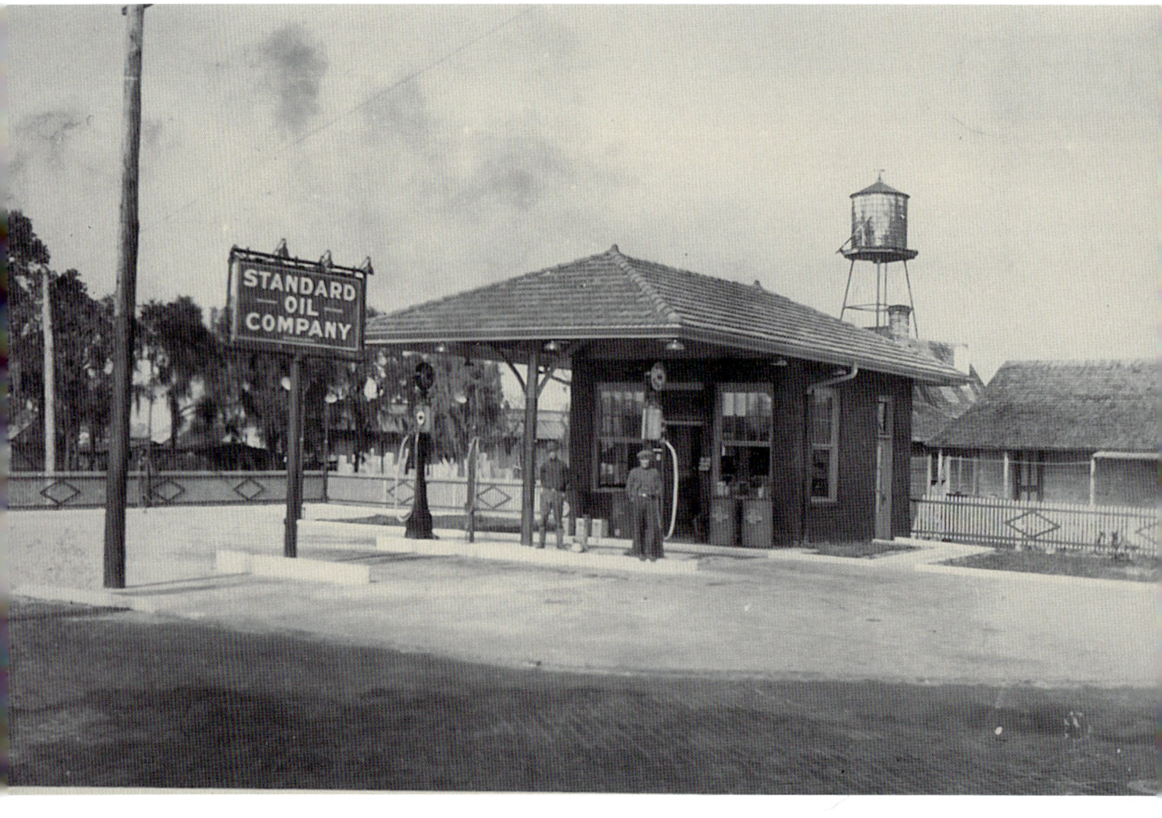

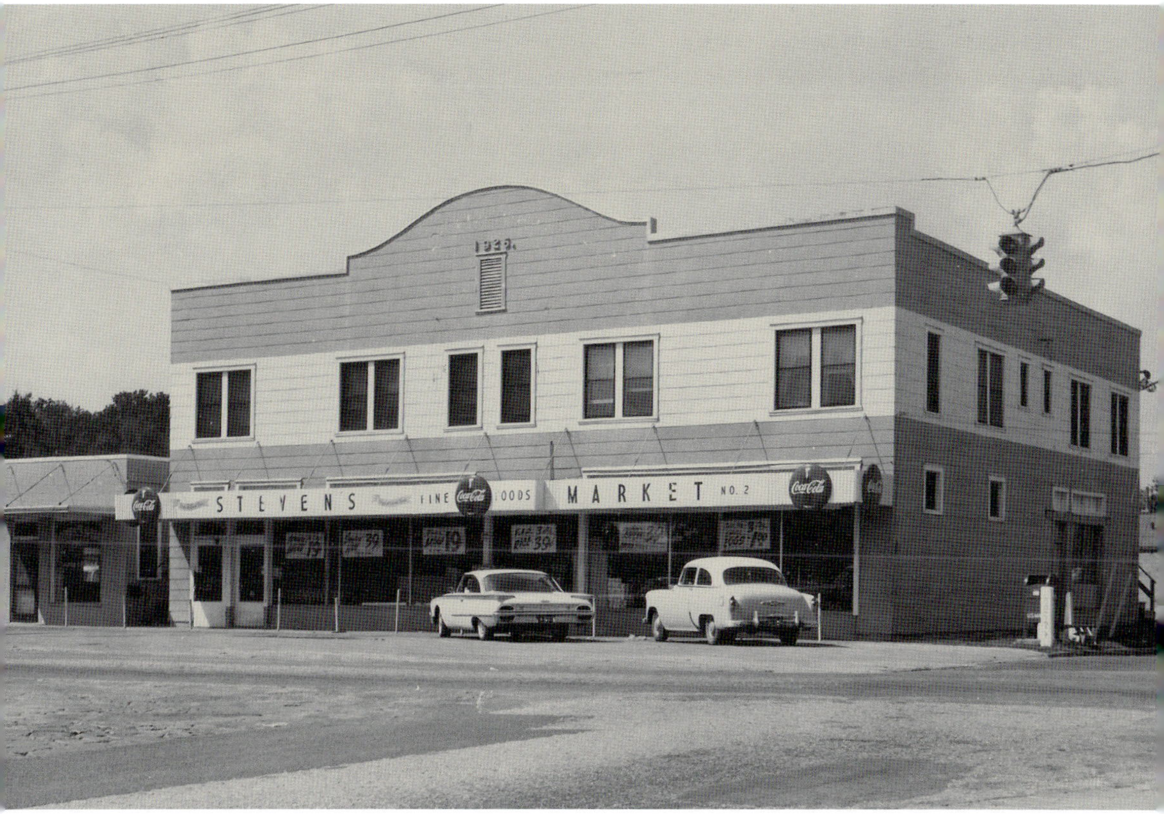

Smith Brothers moved into its handsome new home at the southwest corner of Collins and Alsobrook Streets in 1926. The building was two stories with apartments on the second floor. Located in the single-story building on the south side was a barbershop, which was owned and operated by Henry J. Robinson. The 1960s photograph of Steven's Market No. 2 advertised bread at 19¢ per loaf, and eggs were three dozen for $1. Today it is the site of Waller's Power Equipment, which was originally founded in 1926 as Wright Furniture Hardware before changing its name to WPE in 1954 and moving to this location in the 1960s.

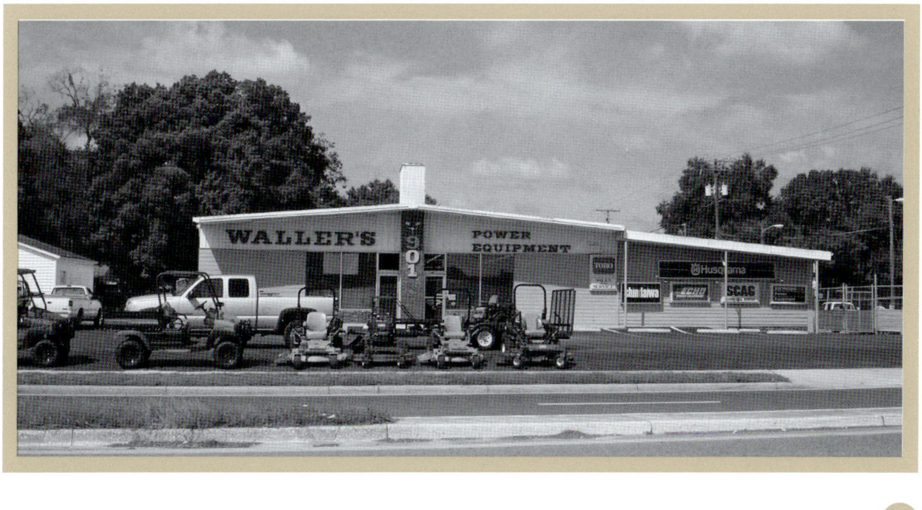

As the town edged further south, the Plant City Mall was built in the middle 1960s. Eckerd Drugs, Grants Department Store, Publix Market, Sears, and various other businesses moved to this new location. A new movie theater replaced the longtime Capital Theater located downtown. Storefronts have come and gone, and the movie theater is no longer there. Now anchored by Big Lots discount store and Save-A-Lot on the respective north and south ends of the shopping center, the marquee is still proportionate to the original sign.

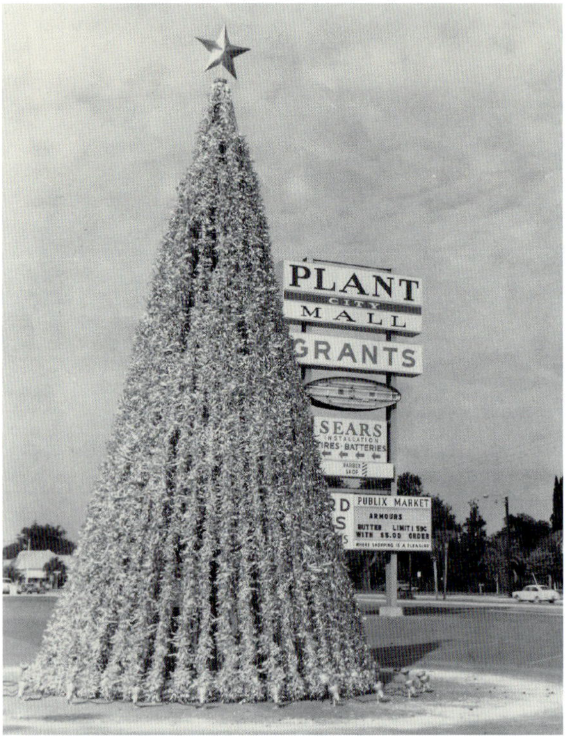

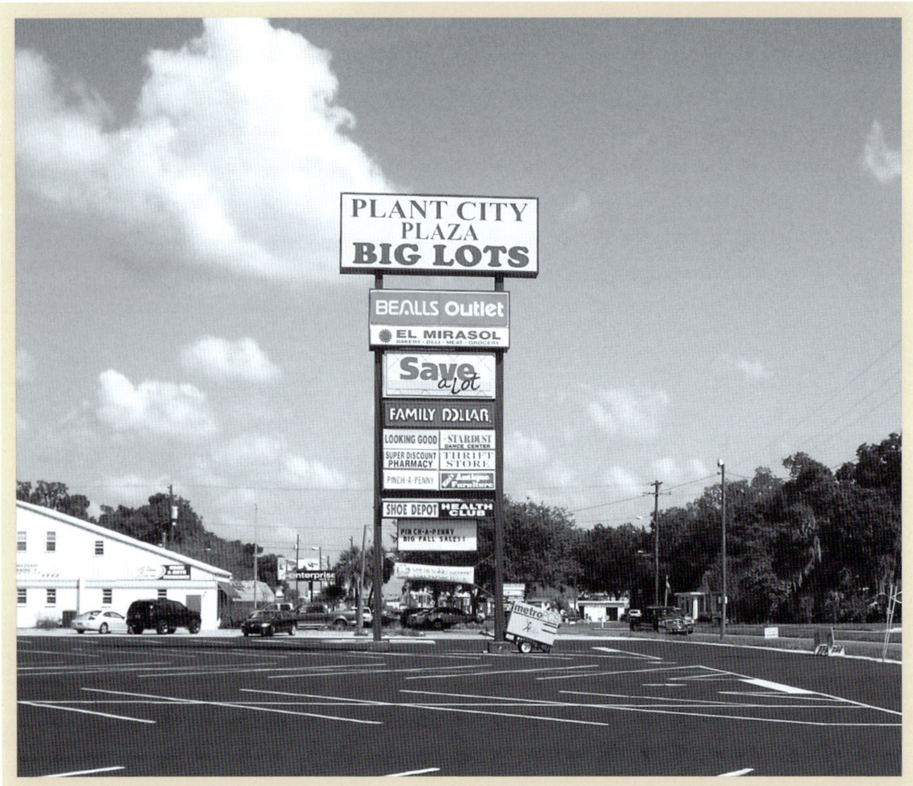

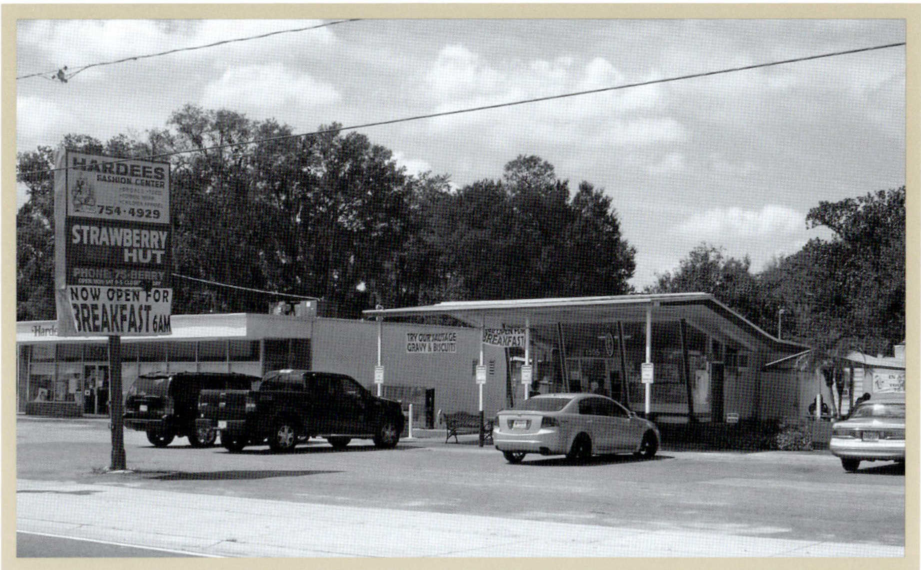

Located on State Road 39 on the north edge of the city, the Super-Test gas station had bulk motor oil, full-service station attendants ready to check the oil and water levels, and pump gas for one's automobile. The small square-block structure with large plate-glass windows was trimmed on the front with Permastone material. The garage structure to the south was demolished in the early 1960s, and one of the first convenience stores in town was built on the site. The old gas station is now the Strawberry Hut sandwich shop, and the store is Hardee's Fashion Center.

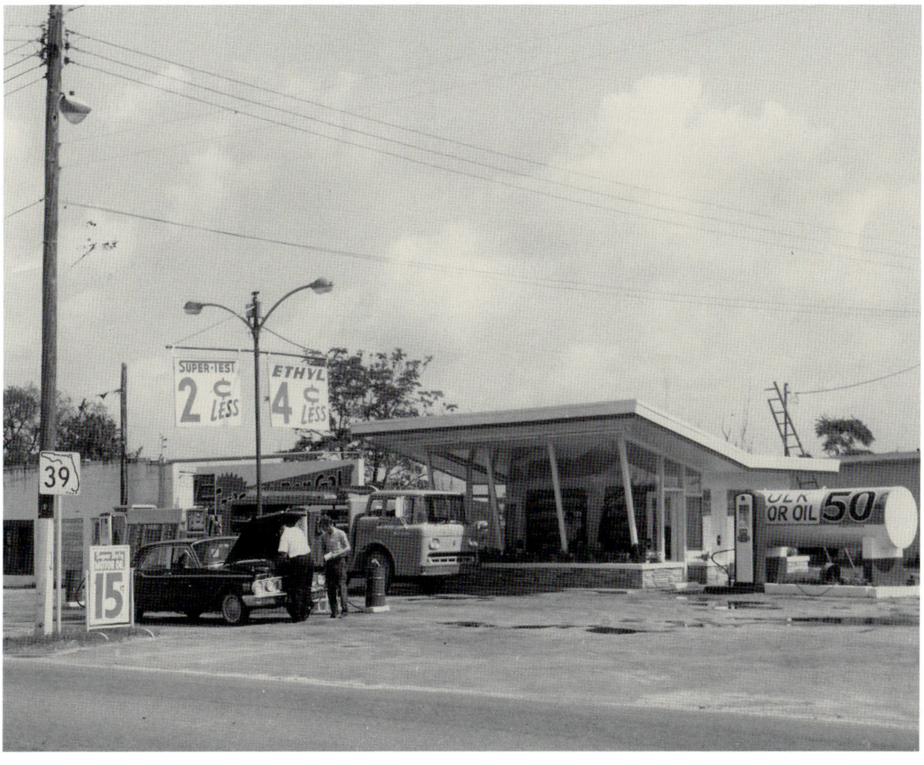

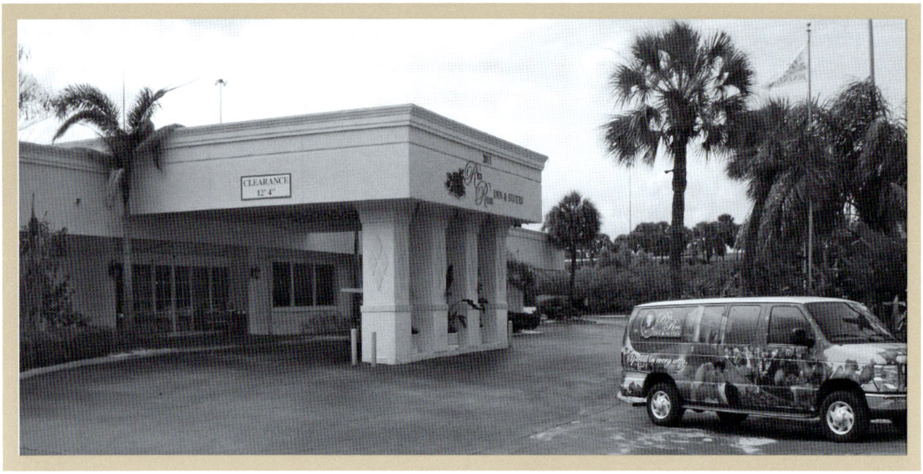

Built in the late 1960s, at the junction of Interstate 4 and State Road 39, the Holiday Inn chain motel included air-conditioning, a swimming pool, a 1776 theme restaurant and lounge, and color televisions in all the rooms. The Red Rose Inn and Suites is Plant City's only full-service hotel and has been extensively renovated to reflect the theme of the nearby historical district areas of homes and businesses.

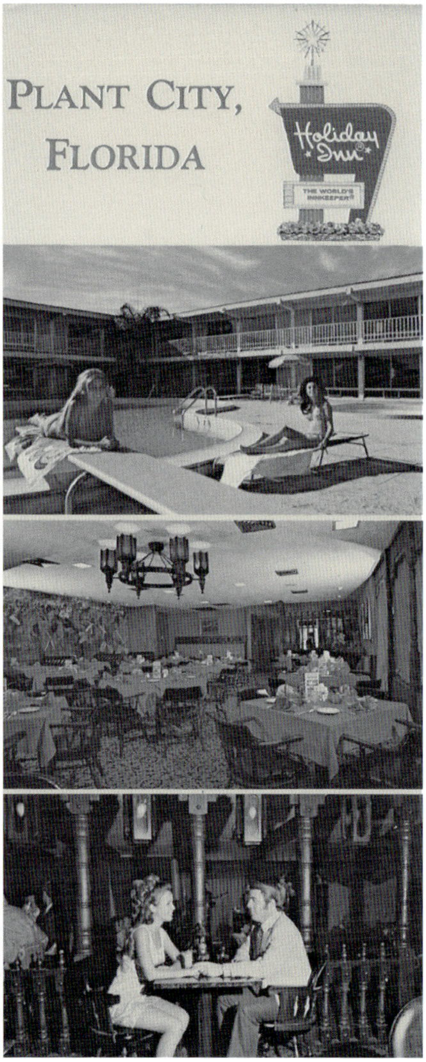

CHAPTER 3

Education

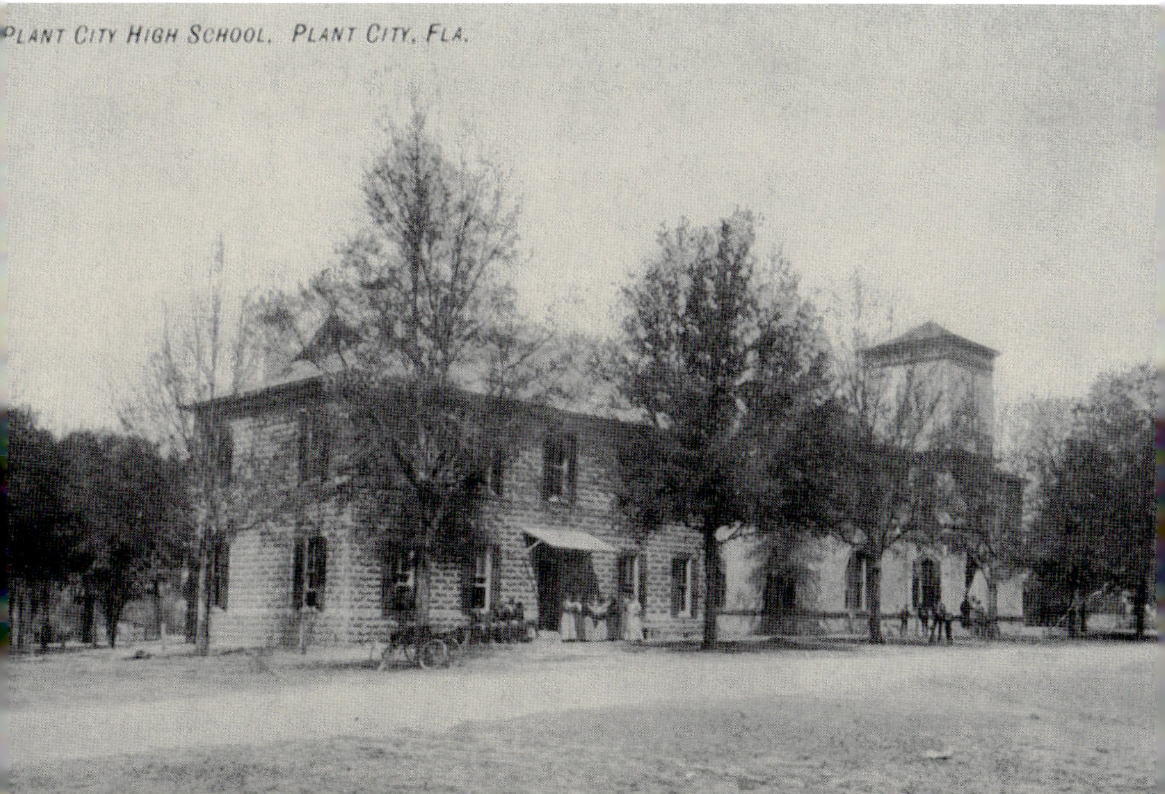

Built in 1893, the Plant City High School building was located on the west side of Wheeler Street near Baker Street. Adjacent to the high school building was the grammar school building, both of which were demolished in 1958 to make way for a new city hall.

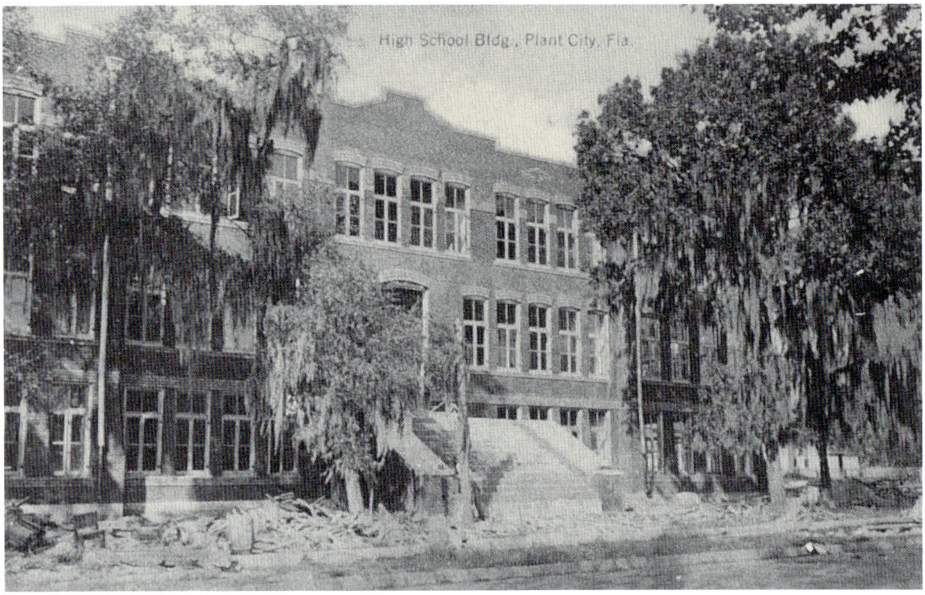

The high school building nearing completion of construction is seen here in a 1915 postcard of the Collins Street front facade before the portico and columns were added. The lawn is still shaded by grand, moss-covered oaks. The 1999 photograph from the East Hillsborough Historical Society's 25th Annual Banquet shows pastry designer Becky Pierce putting the final touches of icing on the building replica cake. In the background is Dorothy Lamb, who provided lovely musical selections on the harp.

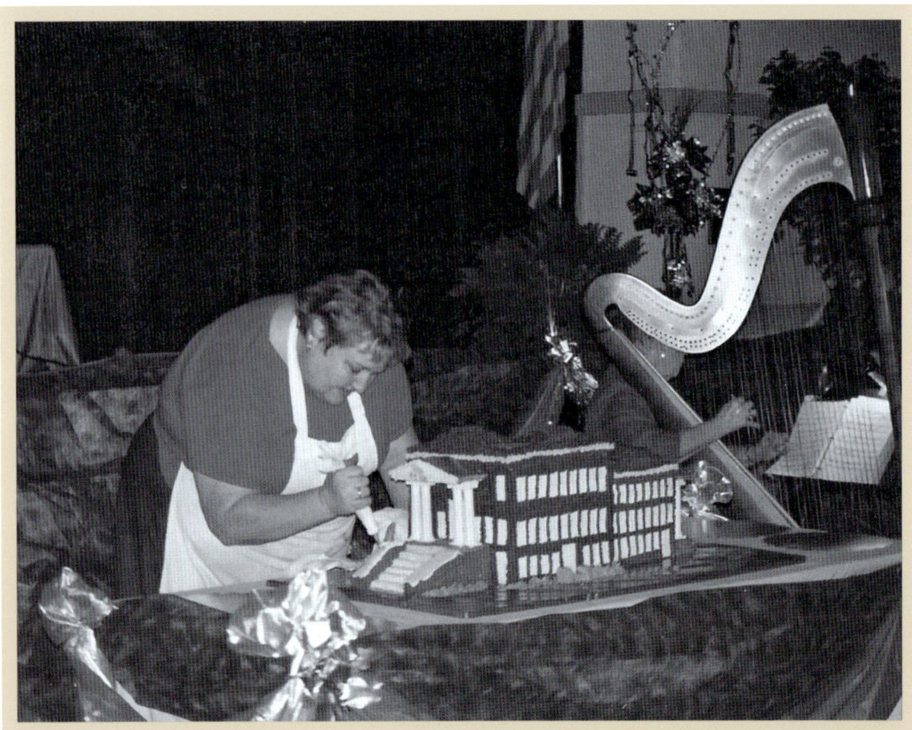

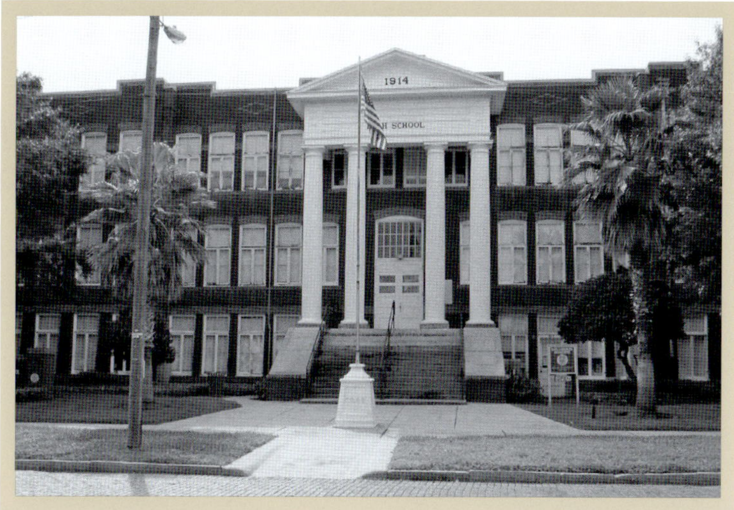

As depicted in this early postcard of the Plant City High School, which was built in 1914, school officials had landscaped and sodded the lawn. The WPA dedicated a flagpole on the front center walk in 1937. Listed on the National Register of Historic Sites, the building is owned by the City of Plant City and is managed by a partnership with the East Hillsborough Historical Society. The society houses its offices, pioneer museums, and its genealogy, family, and local history archives center here. Other displays of agricultural, classroom, photography, and railroad memorabilia are present. The large auditorium is used for community musical and theater productions.

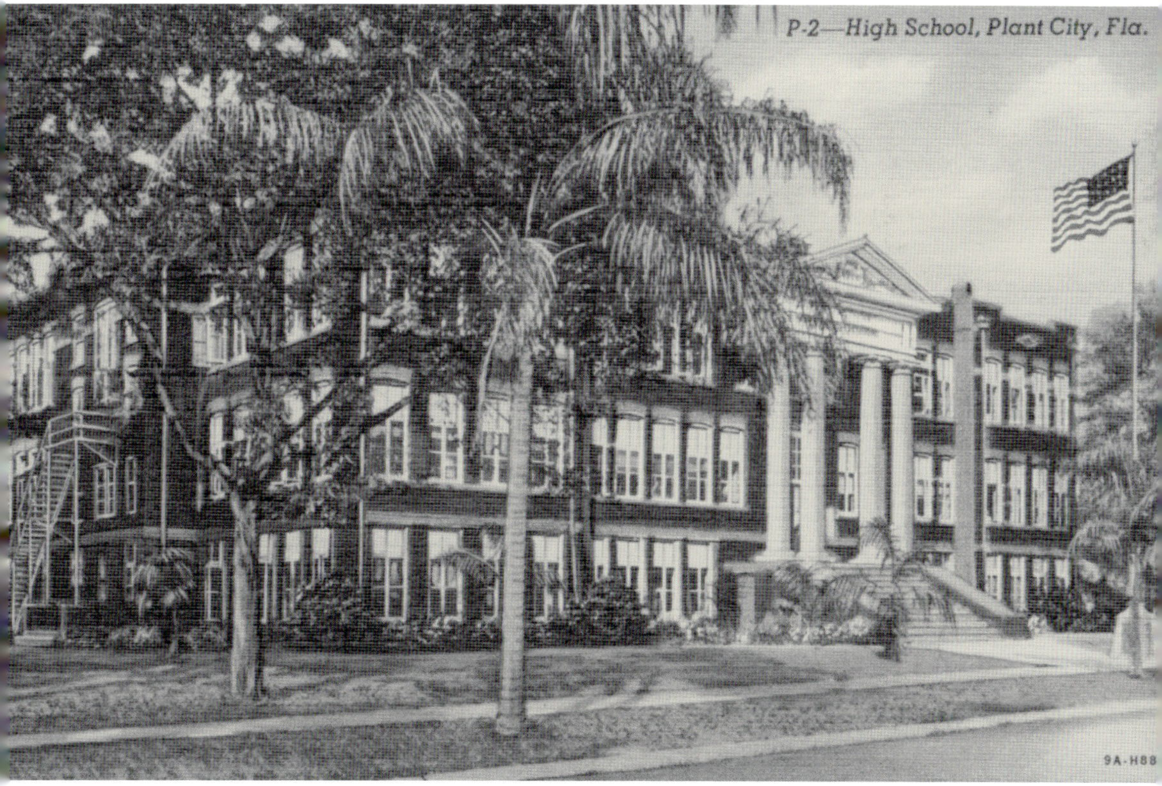

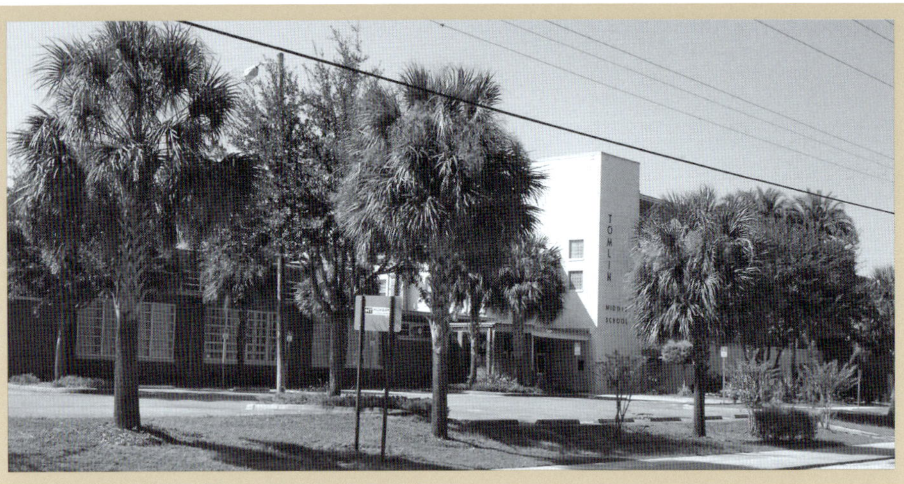

This beautiful Plant City Senior High School, built in 1955, was one of the finest high schools in the South. The modern school building featured a separate auditorium, gymnasium, and band shell.

Converted to Tomlin Middle School in 1973, full-site air-conditioning was completed in 1980. Prior to 1973, Tomlin Junior High School had for many years been located in the 1914 building.

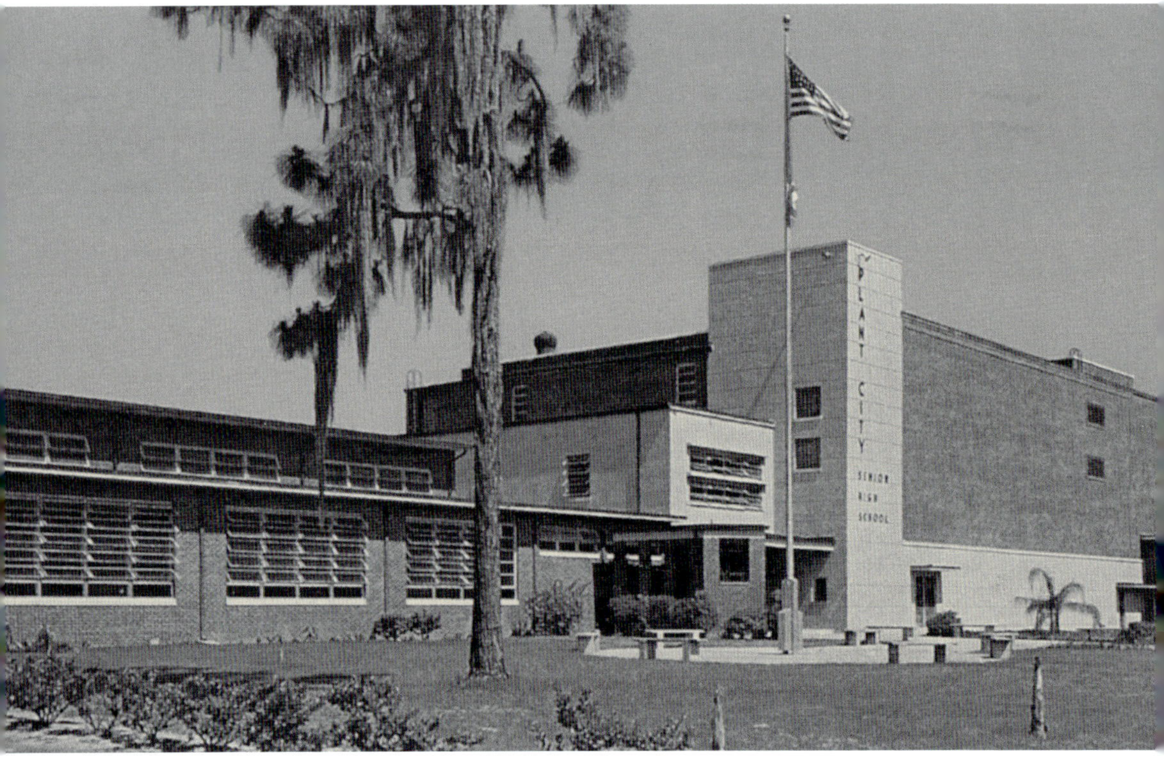

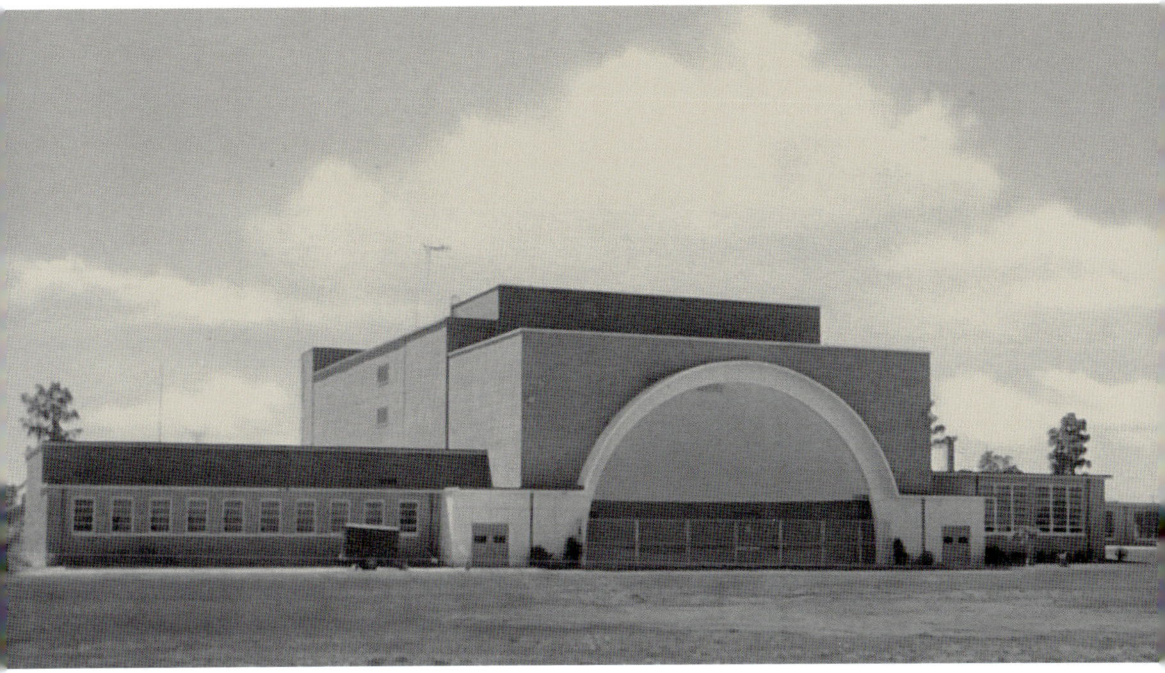

The open-air band shell of the 1955 Plant City High School building was located to the rear of the large auditorium that featured balcony seating and sloping flooring. Rumors of demolition of the band shell created quite a stir amongst the community, thus saving its demise. In 1973, the first graduating class of the newest Plant City High School moved to the single-story brick structure recently built on Alexander Street at the intersection of Maki Road. Having outgrown its physical capacity to handle the student enrollment, additions have been made and newer schools built in the surrounding area.

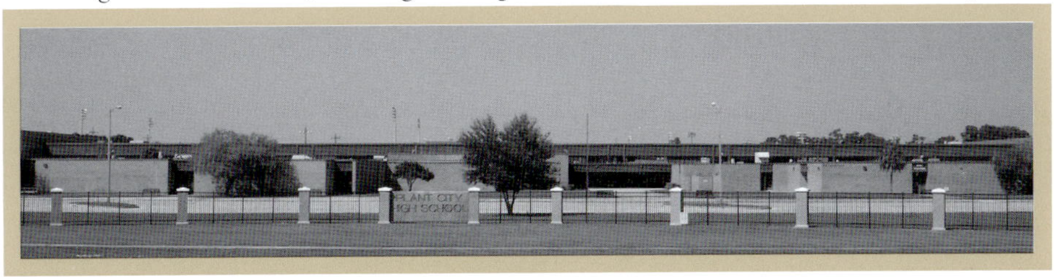

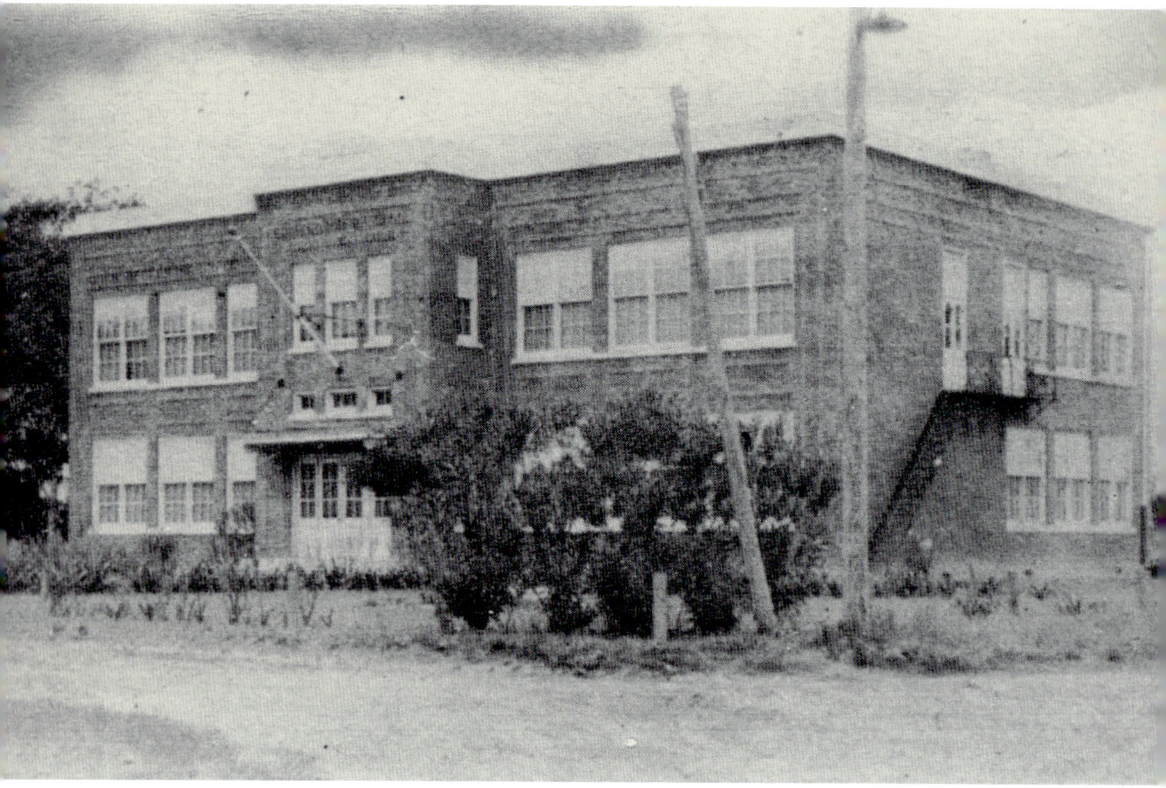

The need for a new elementary school was met with the construction of a new school on South Evers Street in 1923. Named for one of Plant City's earliest teachers, Esther D. Burney School was Plant City's first stand-alone grammar school. Years of community growth in student population have transferred the school from elementary to middle school, then to an alternative education site, and now it once again serves the community as an elementary-level school.

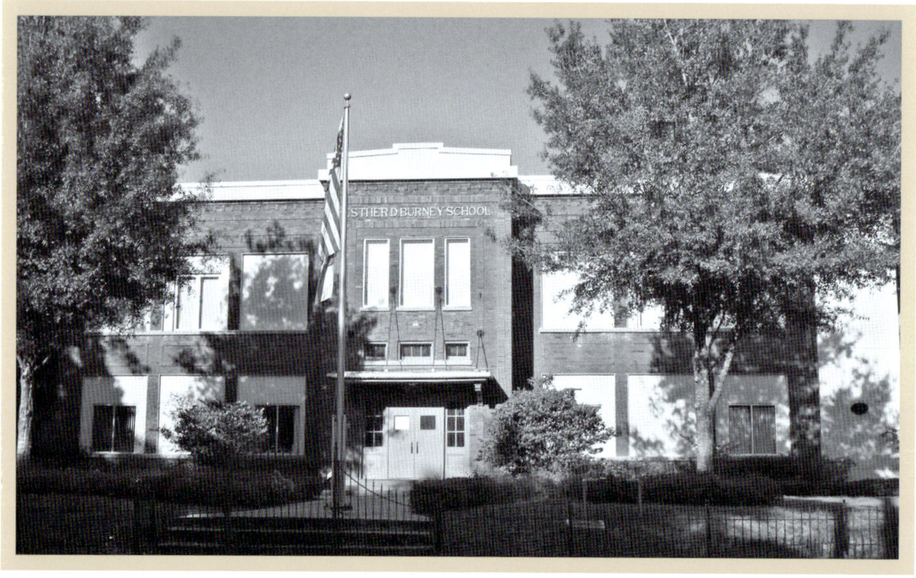

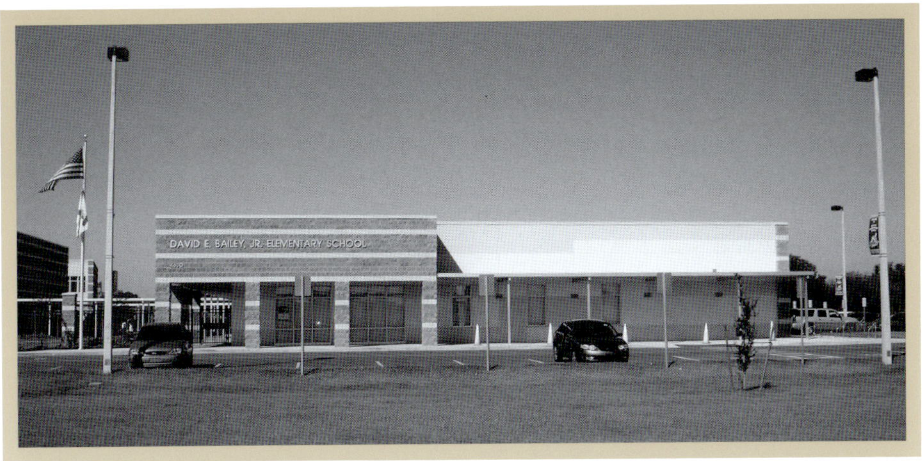

Always with a friendly smile on his face, local educator David E. Bailey Jr. graduated from Plant City High School in 1934 and Florida Southern College in 1939 with a bachelor of science in education degree. He received his graduate and postgraduate degrees from the University of Florida. He truly loved history and was one of the charter members of the East Hillsborough Historical Society. He was honored by the recognition bestowed upon him as Citizen of the Year in 1978 by the local community. The new David E. Bailey Jr. Elementary School in the nearby community of Dover was opened in 2009.

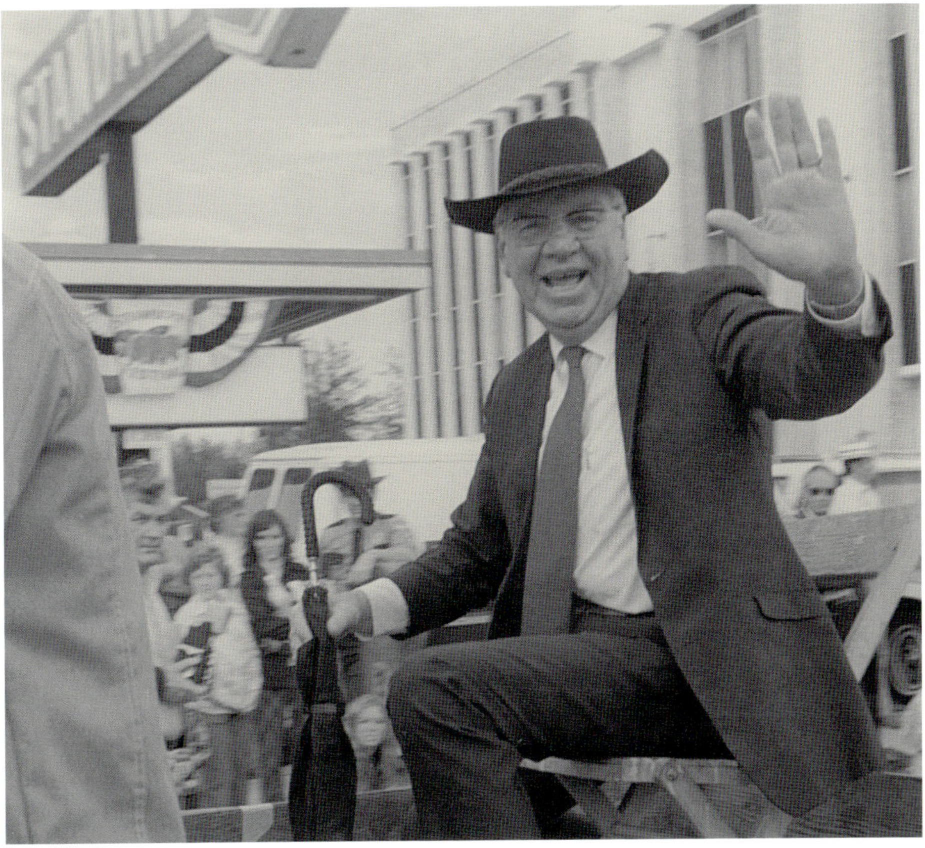

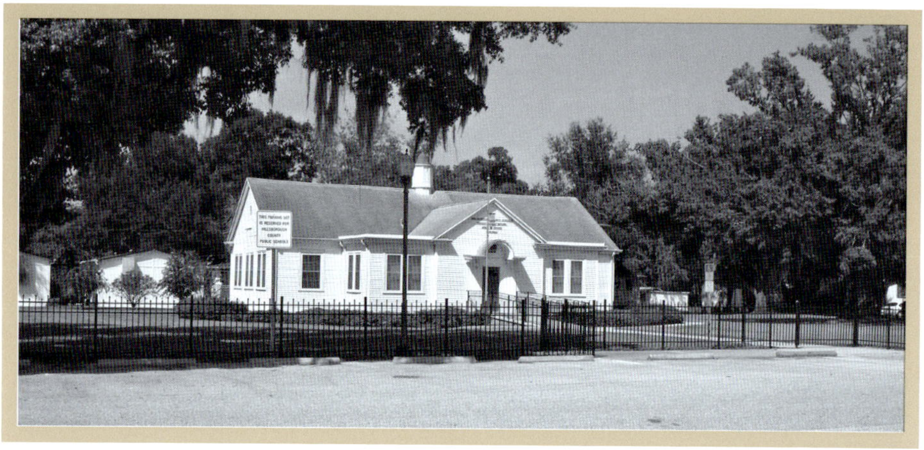

This 1925 Burgert Brothers photograph depicts Courier Field, which was a large green space used for physical education classes for the 1914 Plant City High School; the boys are being coached in football. A banana grove partially covers the livestock's barn, and the agriculture school building is under construction. In 1987, the building was renamed in honor of Dwight M. "Bud" Nifong, who served as an area supervisor of Hillsborough County schools, district supervisor of vocational agricultural education, and an agriculture classroom teacher.

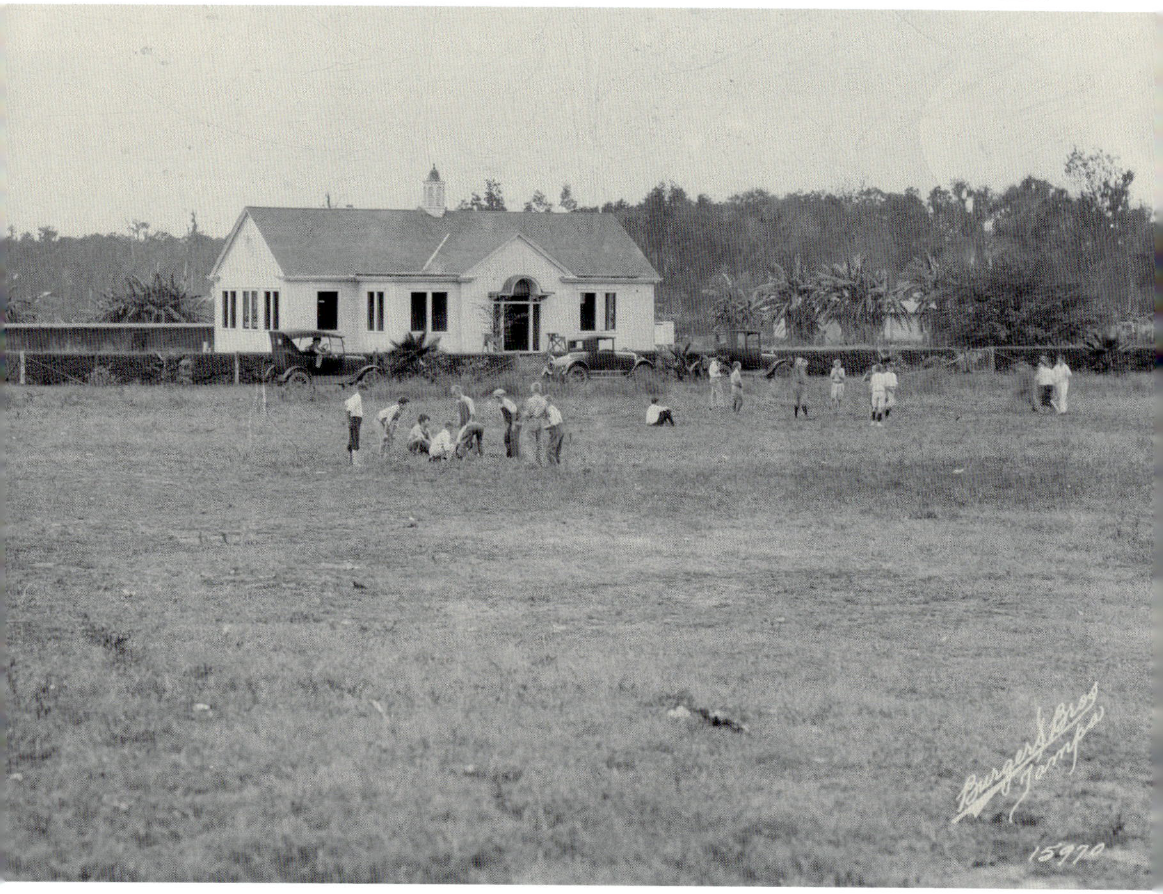

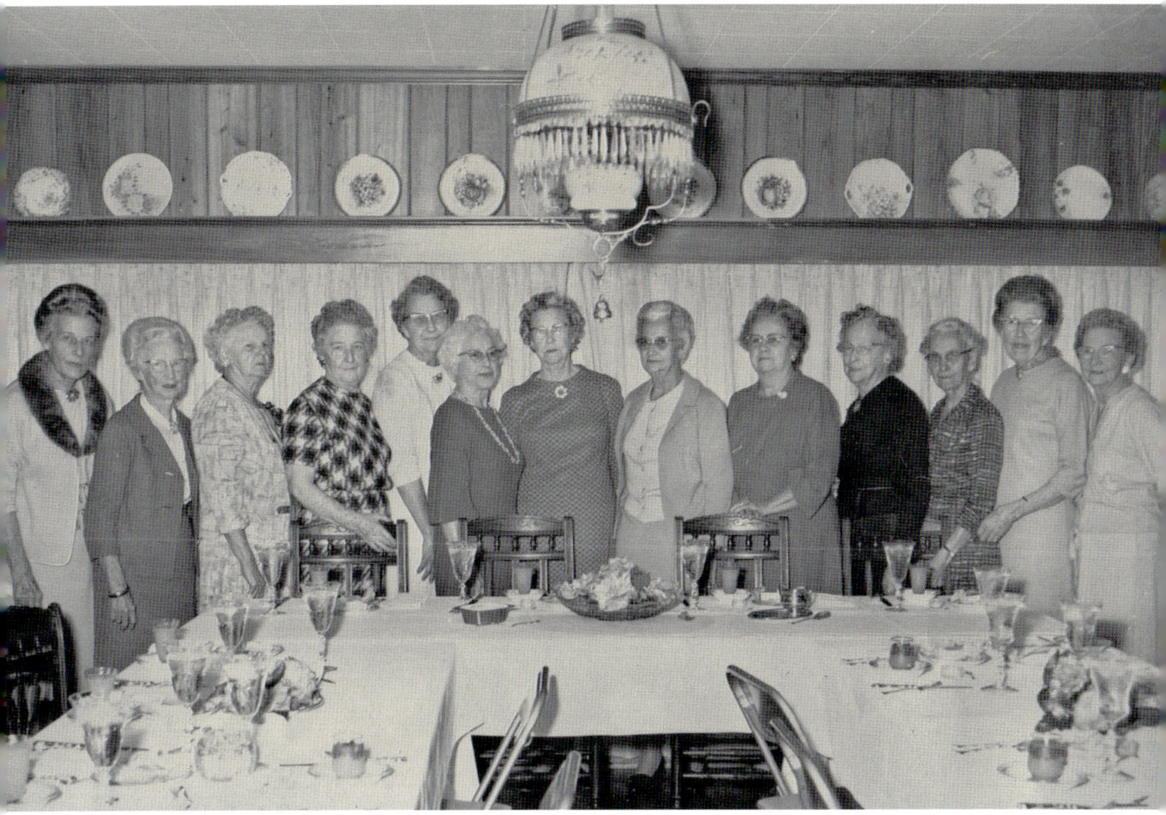

In 1964, the 1914 Plant City High School girls basketball team gathered for an evening of dinner and fellowship at 805 North Wheeler Street and the home of Mrs. J. A. Miles Sr. In 2010, 46 years later, teacher sponsor Danielle Odden and members of the Key Club of the Plant City High School gathered at the same home, now the Strawberry House Bed and Breakfast. This evening of food, fun, and fellowship was in appreciation for their many volunteer hours donated to the East Hillsborough Historical Society at their strawberry shortcake booth.

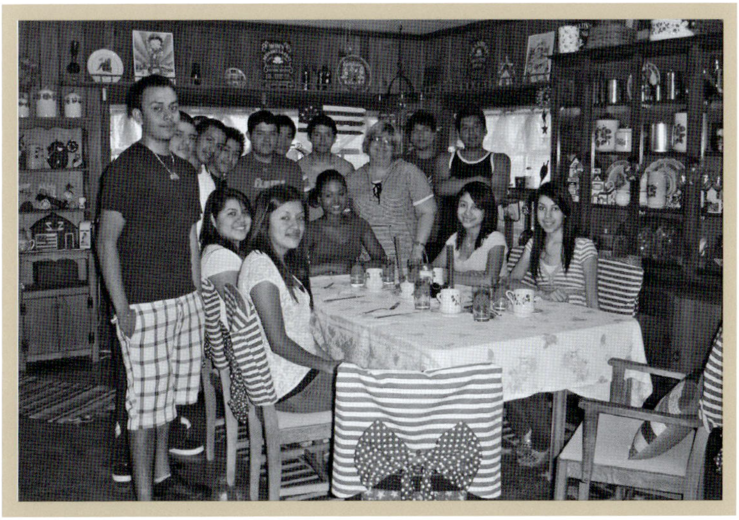

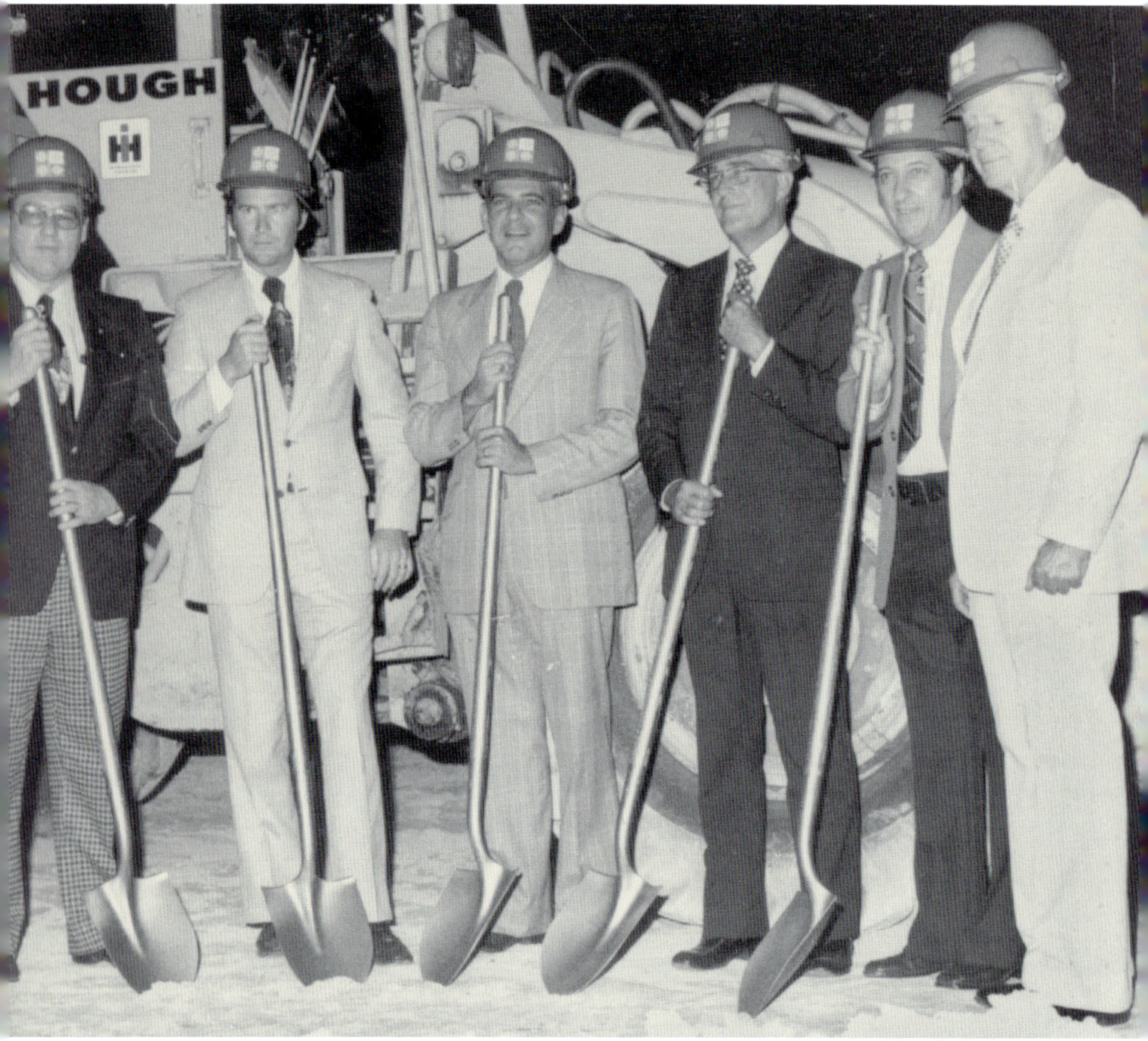

The ground-breaking ceremony for the first permanent building for Hillsborough Community College's Plant City campus was held in 1976. The campus located at 1206 North Park Road is 1 mile south of Interstate 4. This 34-year-old campus has expanded its programs and services to reflect the needs of the community.

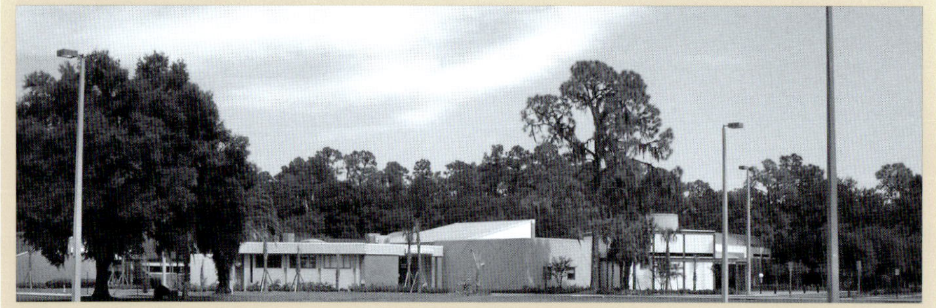

CHAPTER 4

BUILDINGS

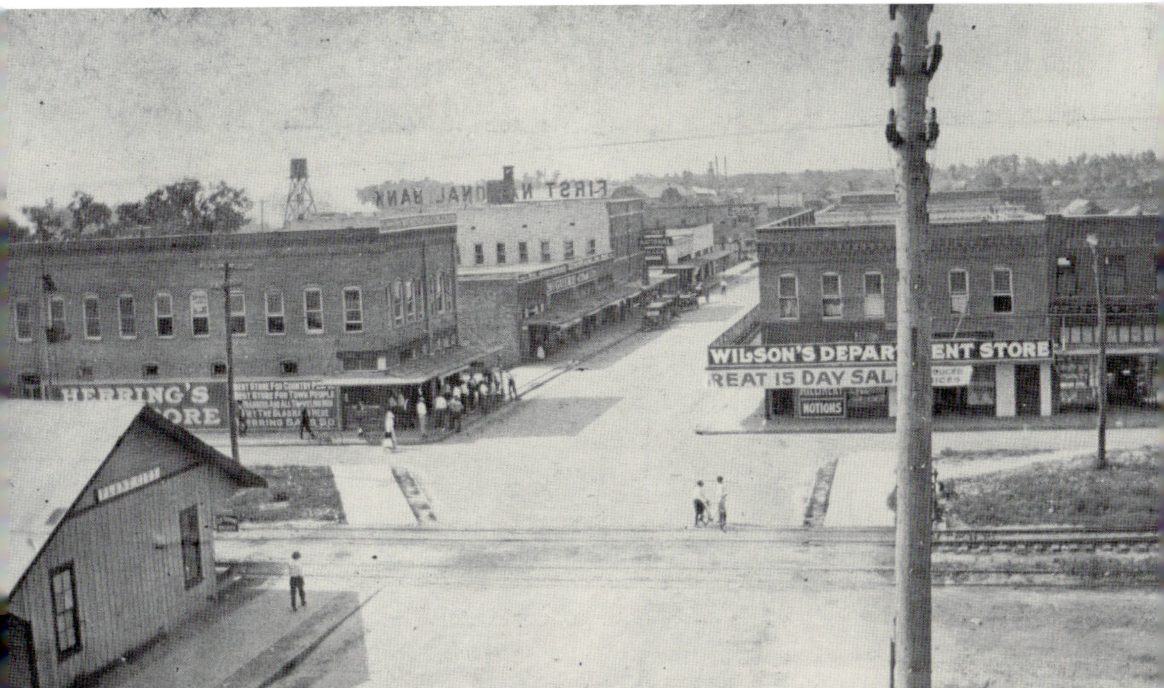

The early 1900s view of Collins Street south at the Coastline Tracks shows the two-story buildings that were occupied by Herring's Drug Store, Wilson's Department Store, and the First National Bank. The single-story building was McGuire's Store. The railway depot had a large sign that read, "Plant City."

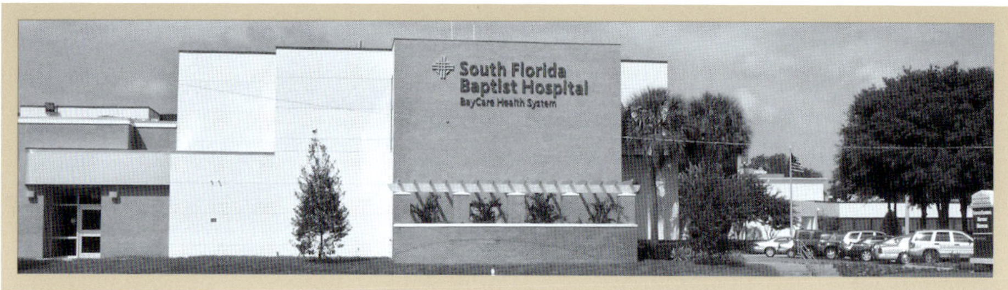

Realizing the need for a larger hospital facility to service the community, leaders and businessmen and businesswomen set out on an endeavor to secure such a place. Not failing, but also not moving along as quickly as the supporters would have liked, the South Florida Baptist Hospital was dedicated in December 1953. Over the last 50-plus years, the hospital has had numerous expansions and again is nearing the completion of a new addition. Now a part of the BayCare Health Systems, South Florida Baptist, located at 301 North Alexander Street, is a 147-bed health care facility.

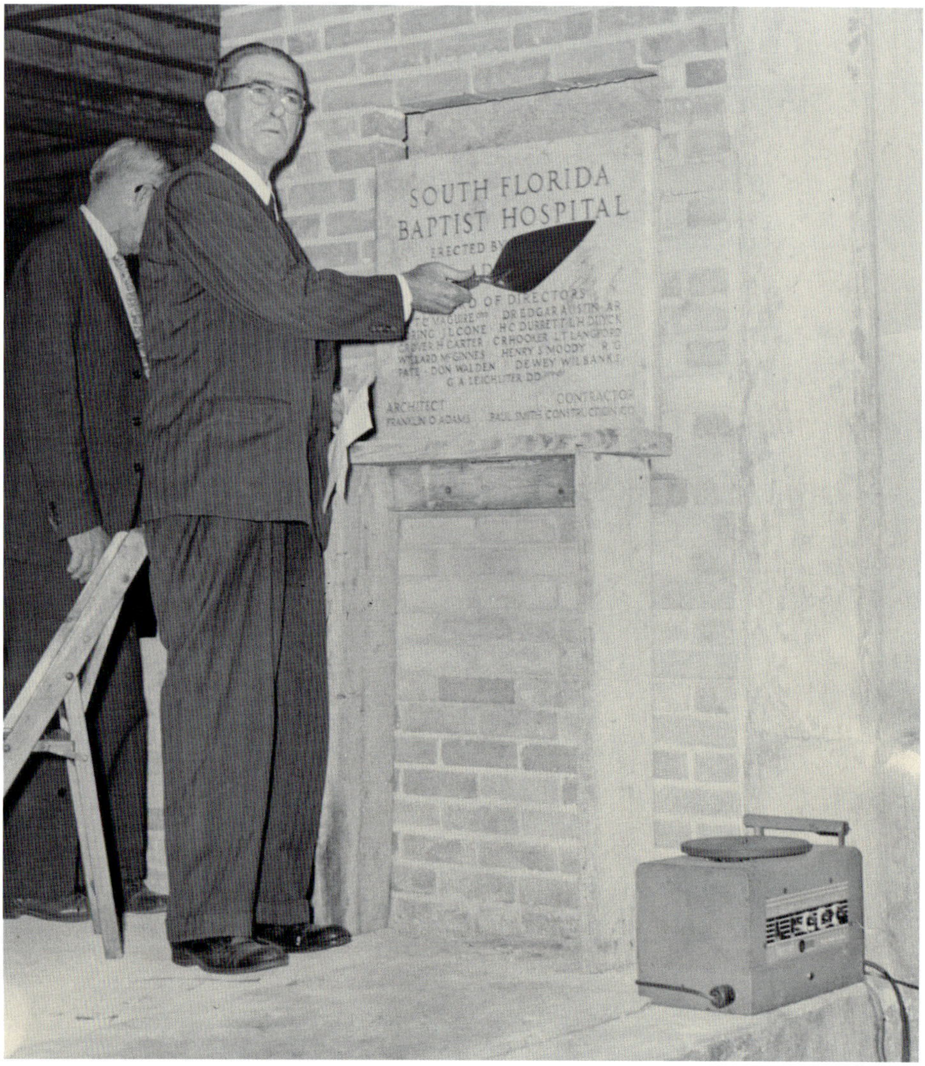

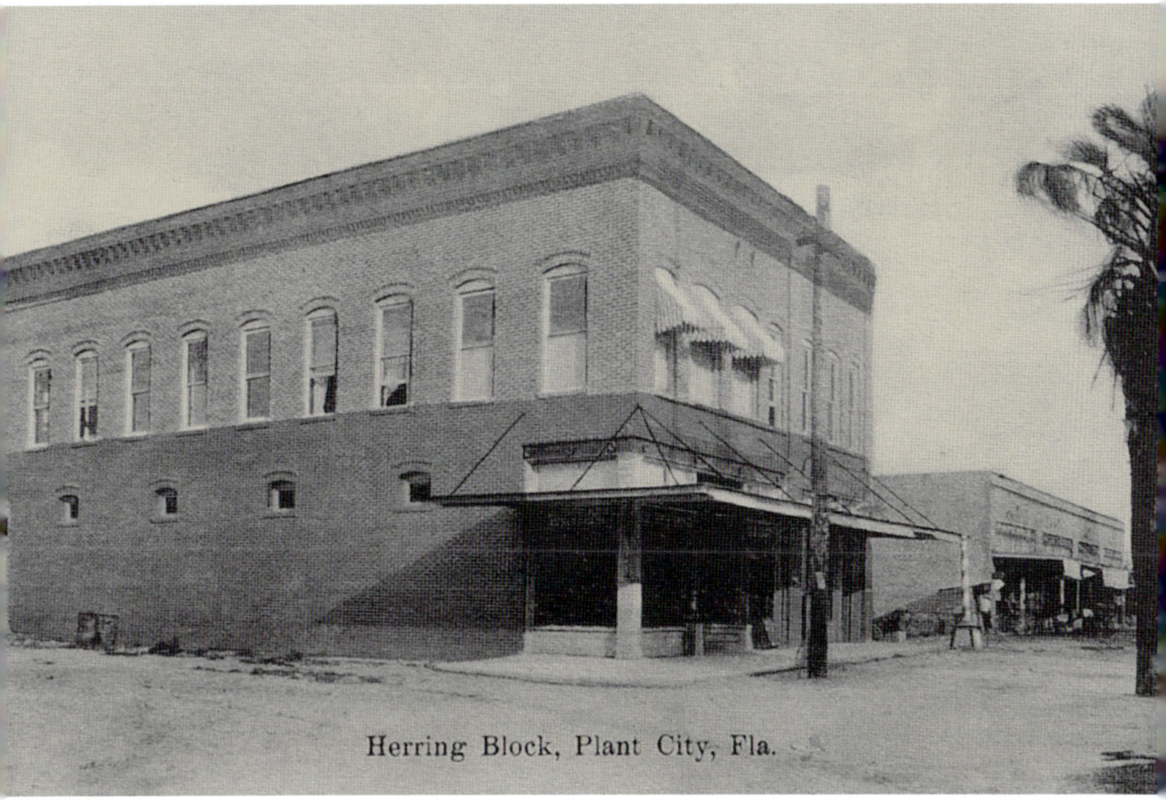

In this 1908 scene at the railway crossing, Herring's Drug Store and the office of J. A. Pearce are visible on the left. Doctors' offices with hospital services were located above Herring's Drug Store. The Herring's Drug Store building is now owned and operated by the Whistle Stop Café. It is rightly named, as trains blow their whistles on the adjacent railway tracks.

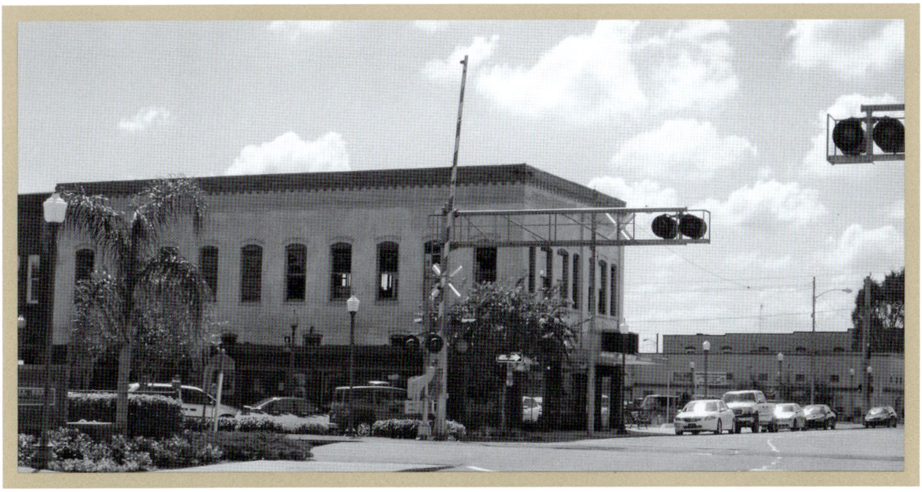

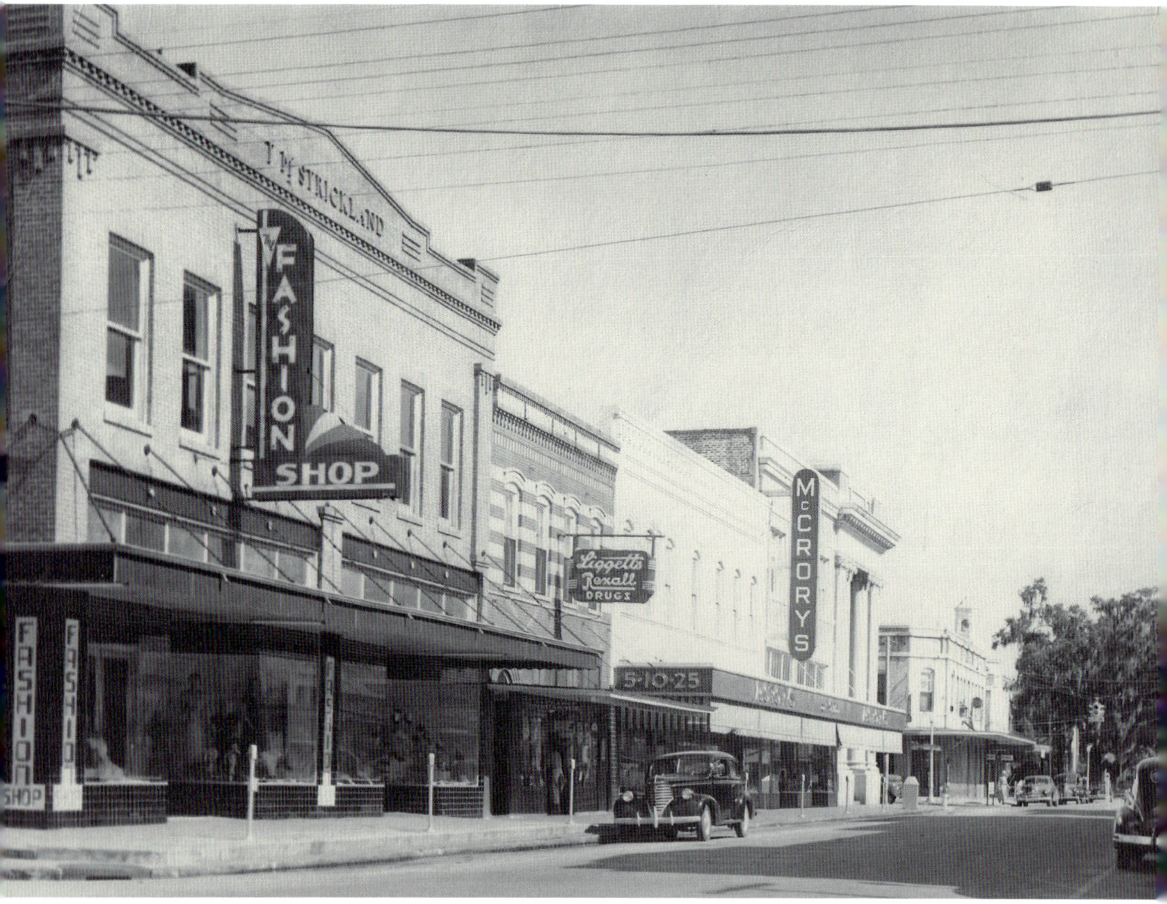

The T. M. Strickland Building, constructed in 1908, was the location of the Fashion Shop, a family apparel store. The interior features a mezzanine, and the children's clothing department was located here in the 1960s. Since the 1970s, the building has been used for commercial offices, including the recent ownership by the Paso Fino Horse Association. The drugstore and five-and-dime stores are antique shops.

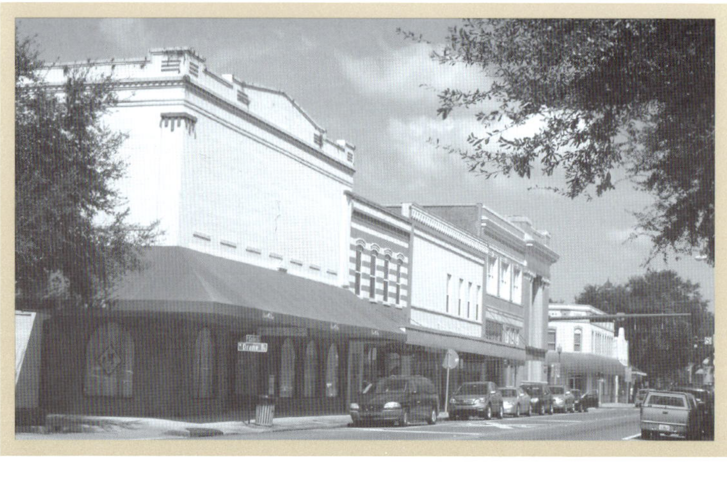

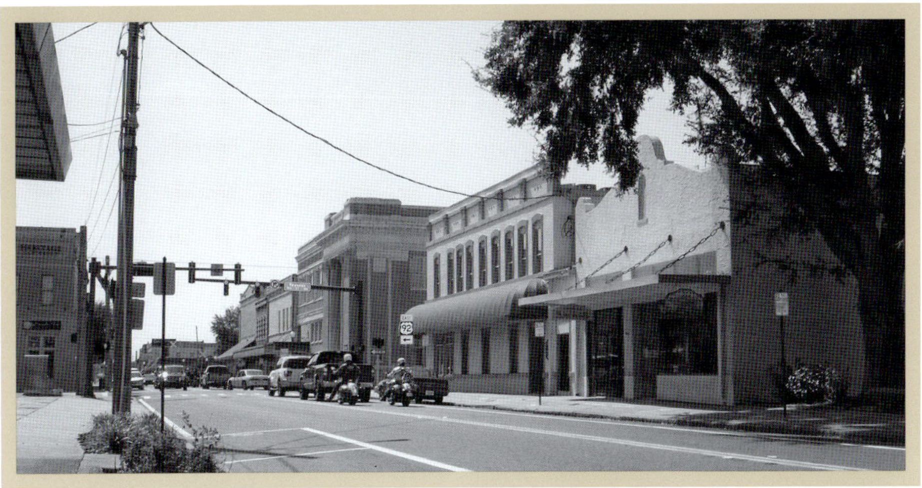

The busy downtown intersection of Collins and Reynolds Streets has long been the hub for local businesses. A closer look reveals that most daily business could be conducted right here at this location. Today the building facades remain virtually the same, but mixed use of retail and office space is experienced. Reynolds Street is now a one-way street with east traffic only.

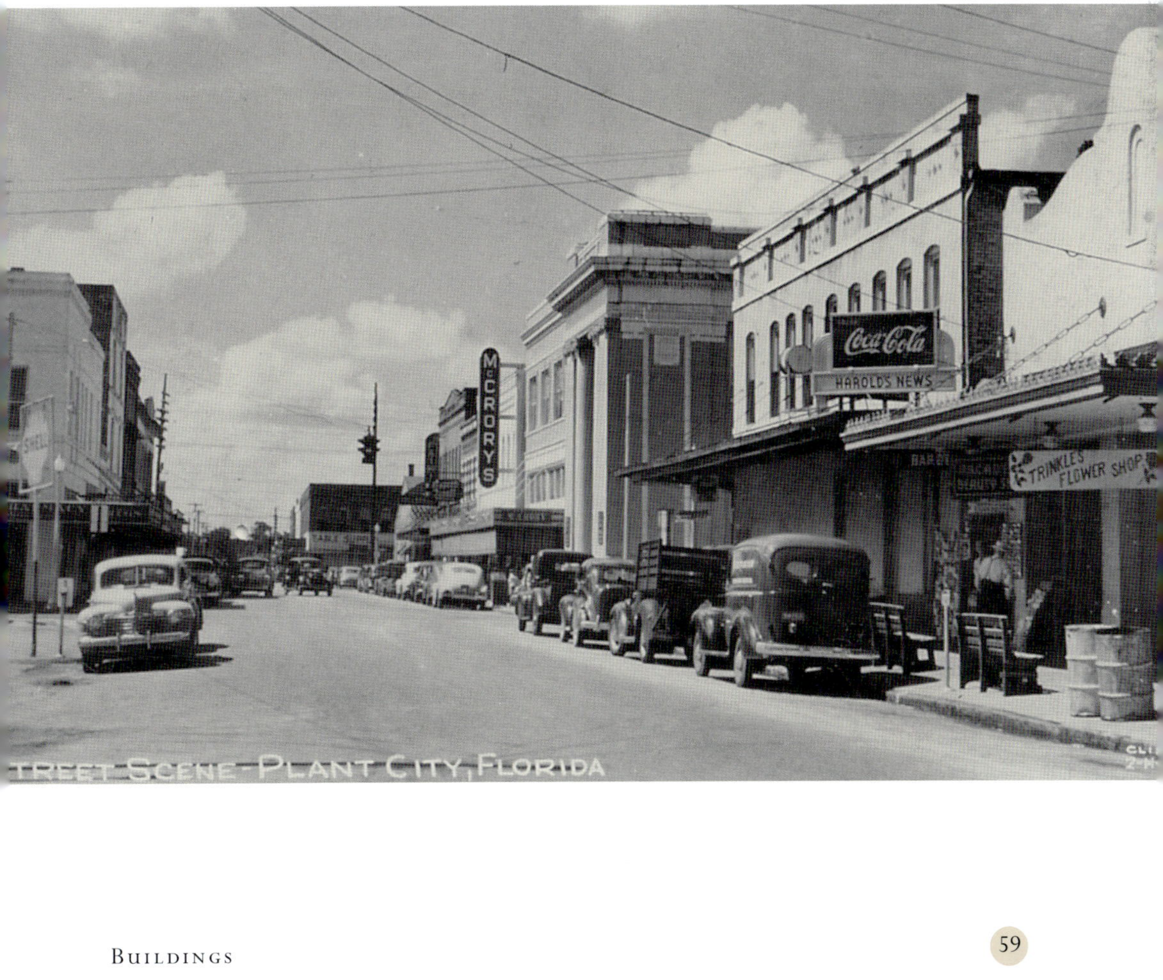

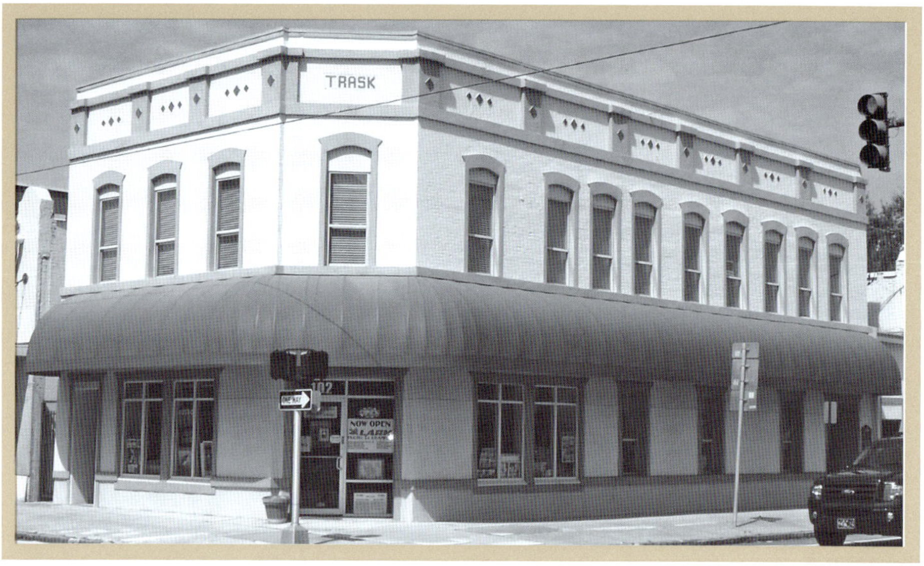

The postcard of the 1908 Trask Building at the corner of Collins and Reynolds Streets has the sign for the post office hanging at the diagonal entryway. A laundry facility, grocery, and music store also occupied the building. The Magnolia Pharmacy was located there soon after, and in 1930 a tile floor was added. A pharmacy remained here until recent years, and the building now has law offices on the second floor with Lark Photography on the ground floor.

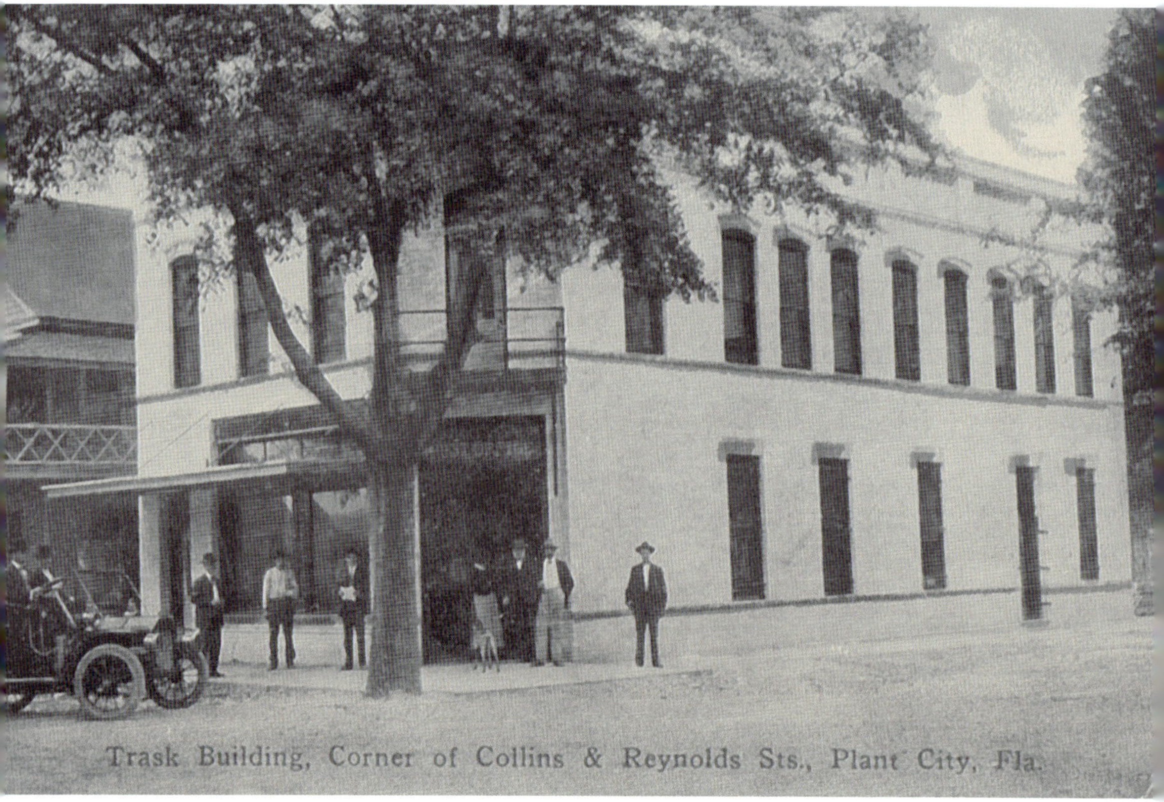

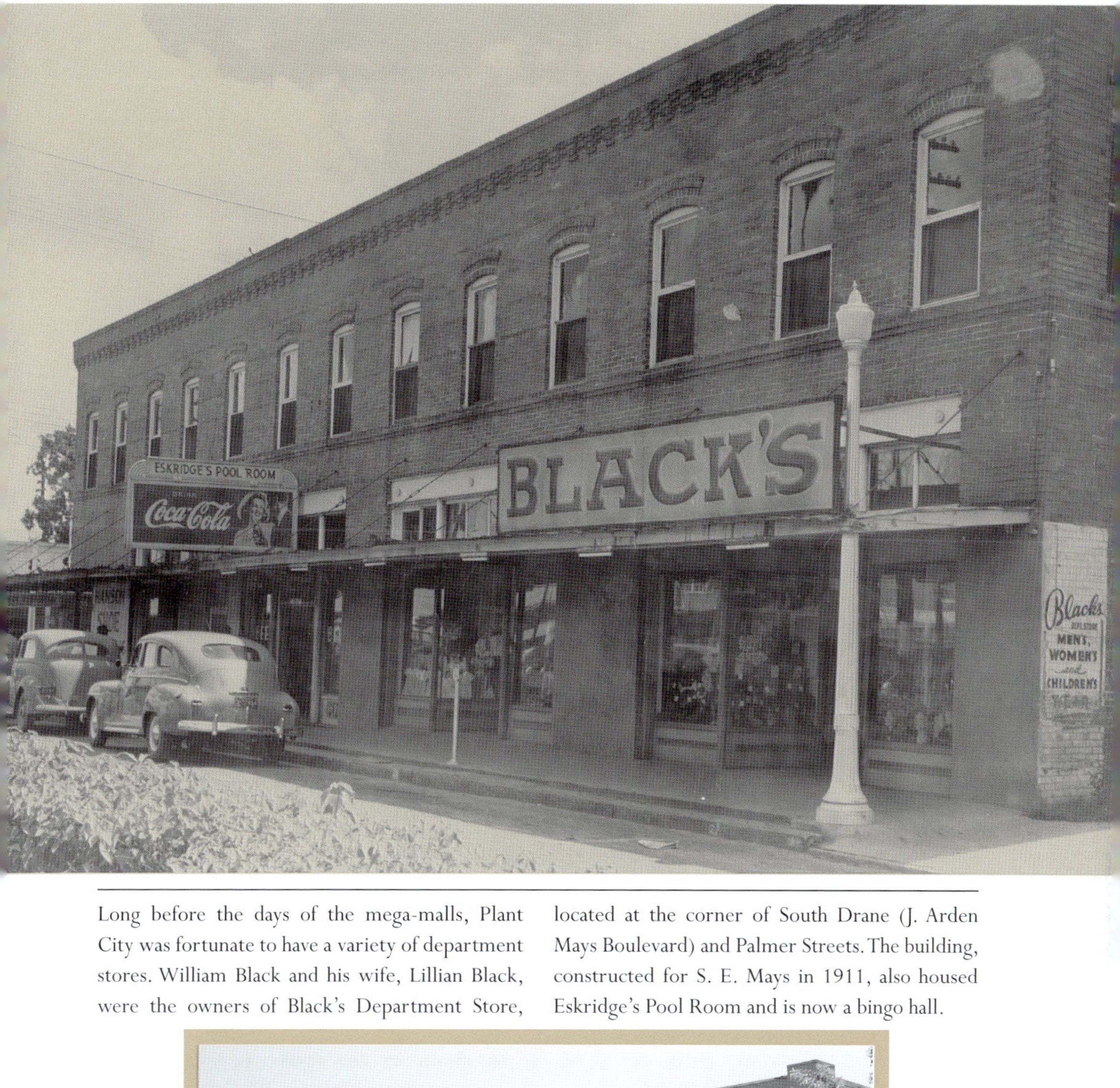

Long before the days of the mega-malls, Plant City was fortunate to have a variety of department stores. William Black and his wife, Lillian Black, were the owners of Black's Department Store, located at the corner of South Drane (J. Arden Mays Boulevard) and Palmer Streets. The building, constructed for S. E. Mays in 1911, also housed Eskridge's Pool Room and is now a bingo hall.

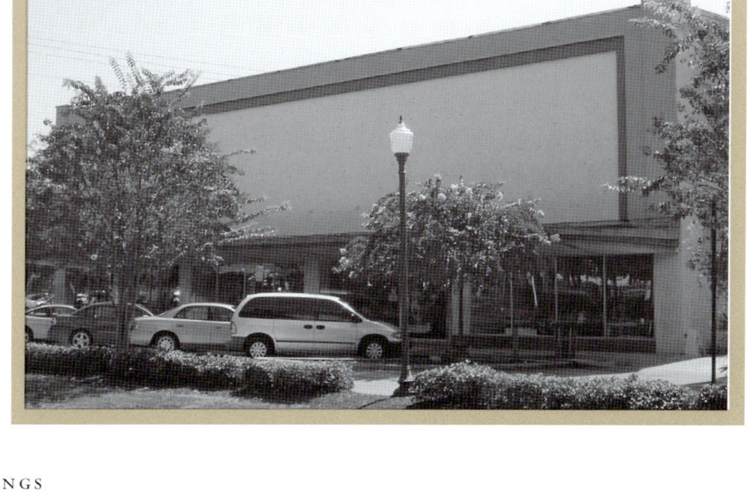

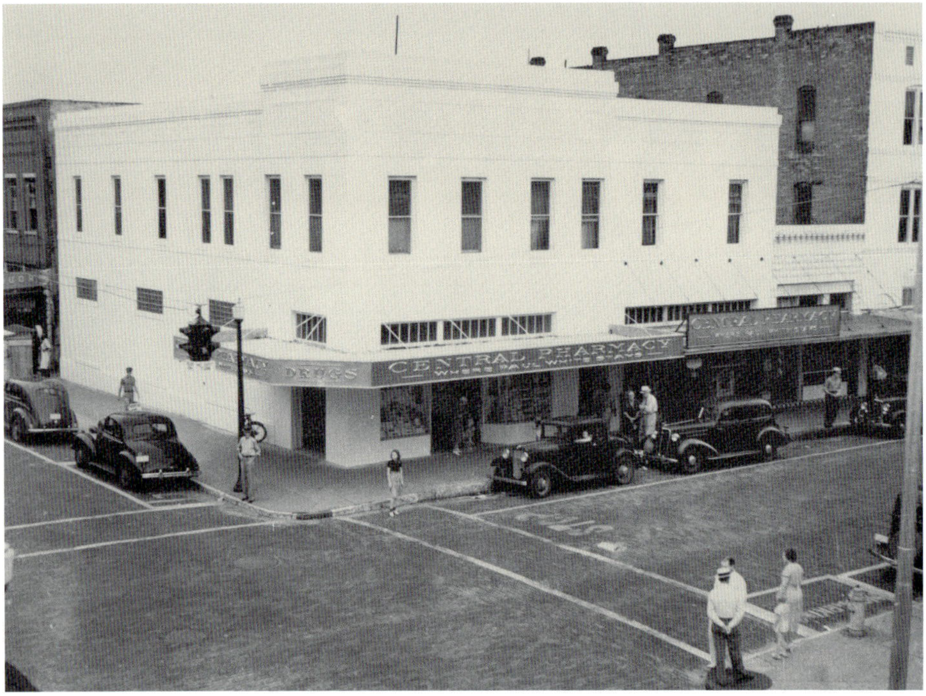

The Central Pharmacy was one of Plant City's downtown pharmacies. Built as the Bank of Plant City, the Central Pharmacy shifted from the corner to a south location before going back to the corner following the closing of the Bank of Plant City during the Great Depression. Upstairs was the Plant City Hospital, which closed its doors when the new South Florida Baptist Hospital opened in 1953. A more recent renovation to the building by the Heritage Law Group and Camellia Rose Tea Room & Gifts has enclosed the facade that once allowed entry from either street front.

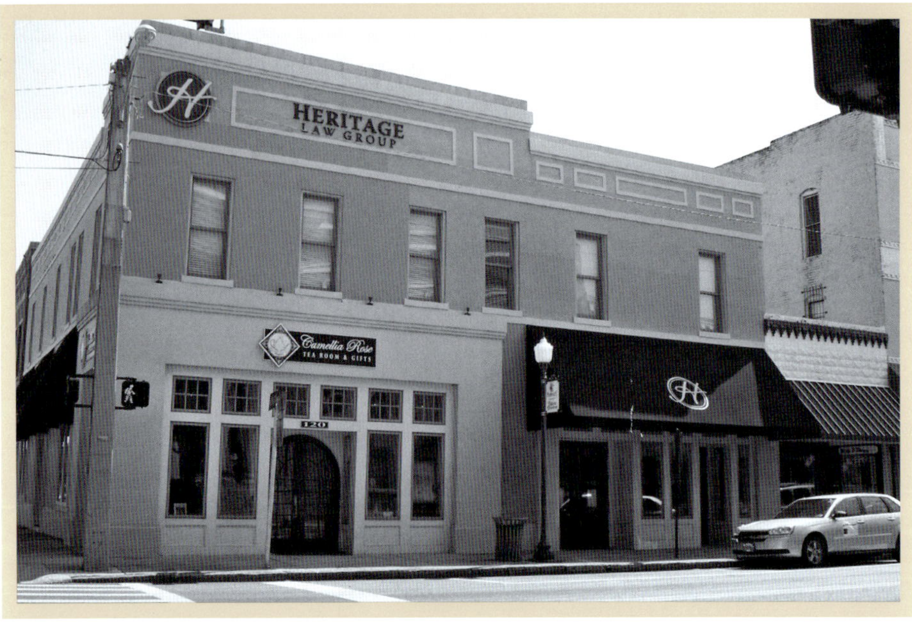

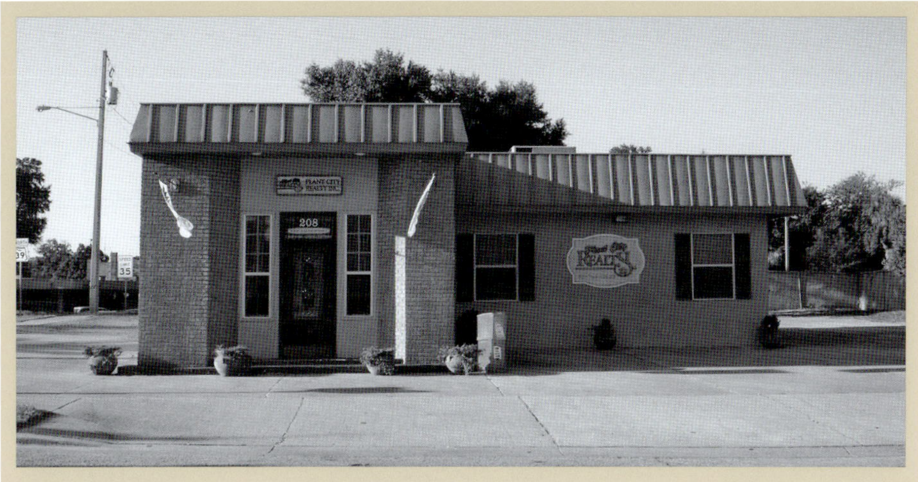

Built in 1938, Jesse E. Ellis was the proprietor of the Sinclair station at the northeast corner of Wheeler and Baker Streets when this photograph was taken in 1954. The Coca-Cola drink box, with the rack of wooden crates and glass bottles, is a scene of the past. The site remained a service or repair station until it was purchased and remodeled as offices for Plant City Realty, Inc.

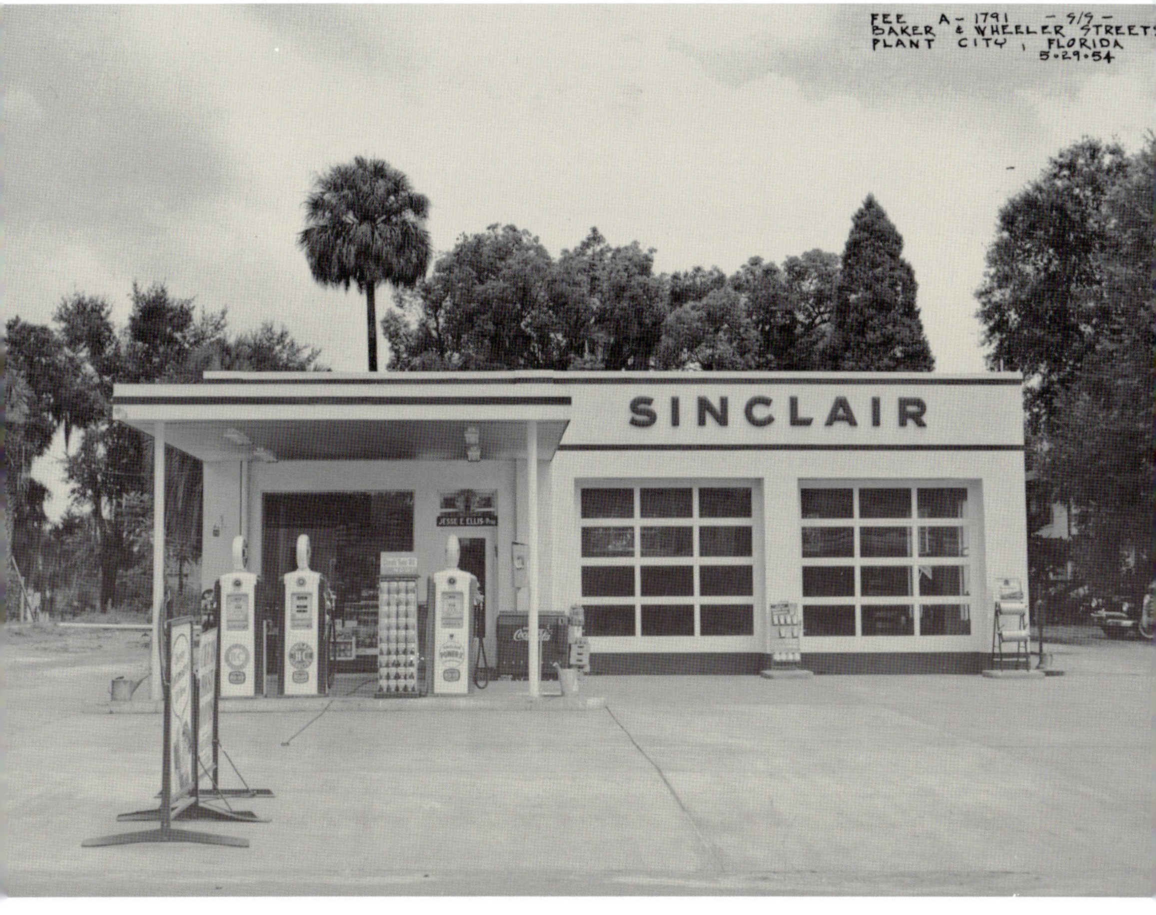

Completed in 1923, the First Baptist Church is the cornerstone building of Plant City's Downtown Commercial Historic District and is located at the southwest corner of Baker and Collins Streets. This classical revival-style structure features two colossal porticos that overlook both streets and is now home to the Cornerstone Center Inc., a nonprofit organization dedicated to the preservation of the property. Although the church built a new sanctuary within the last few decades on the southwest corner of Herring and Palmer Streets, plans are already underway to relocate to recently purchased property on James L. Redman Parkway South.

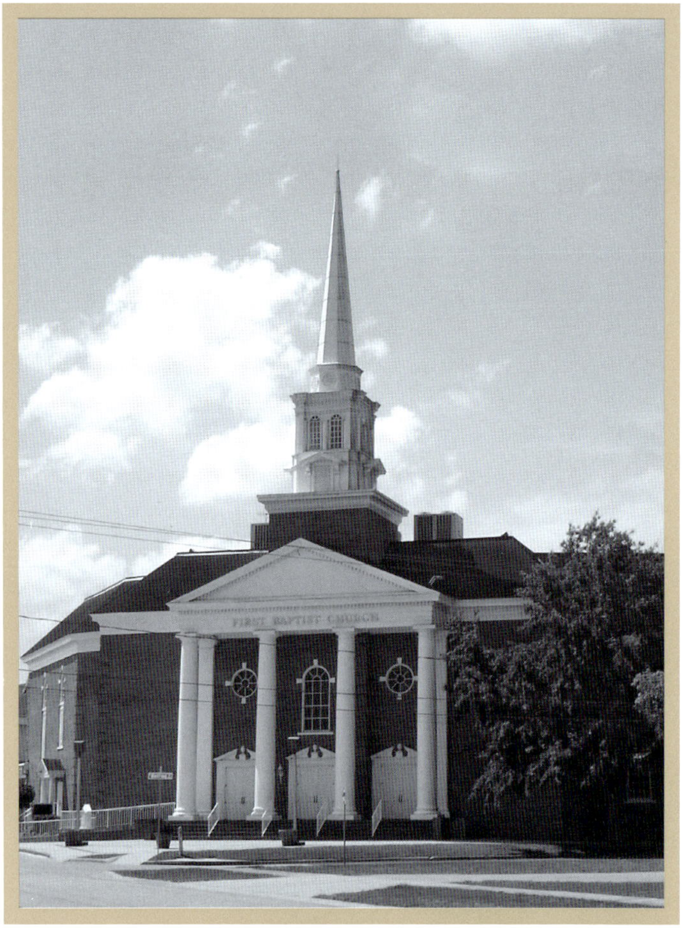

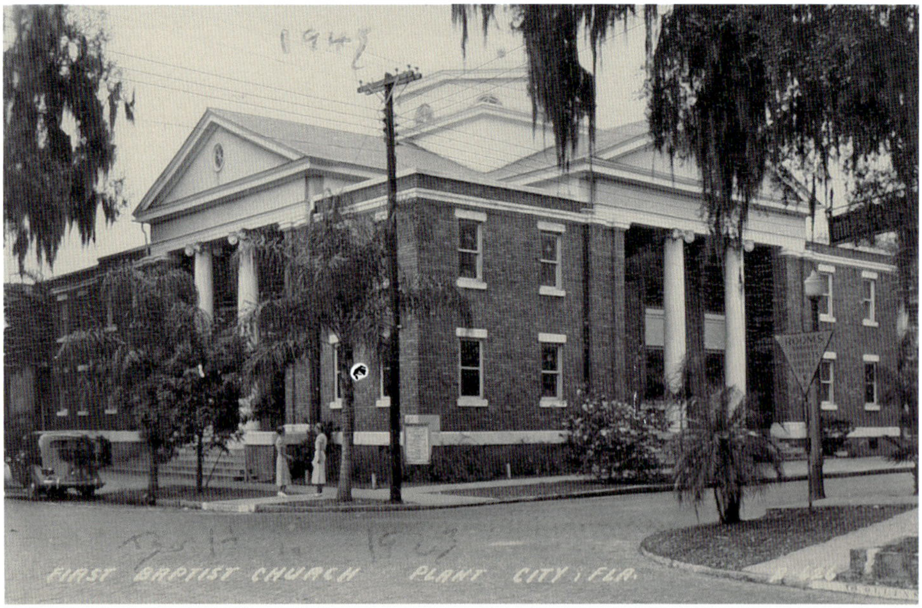

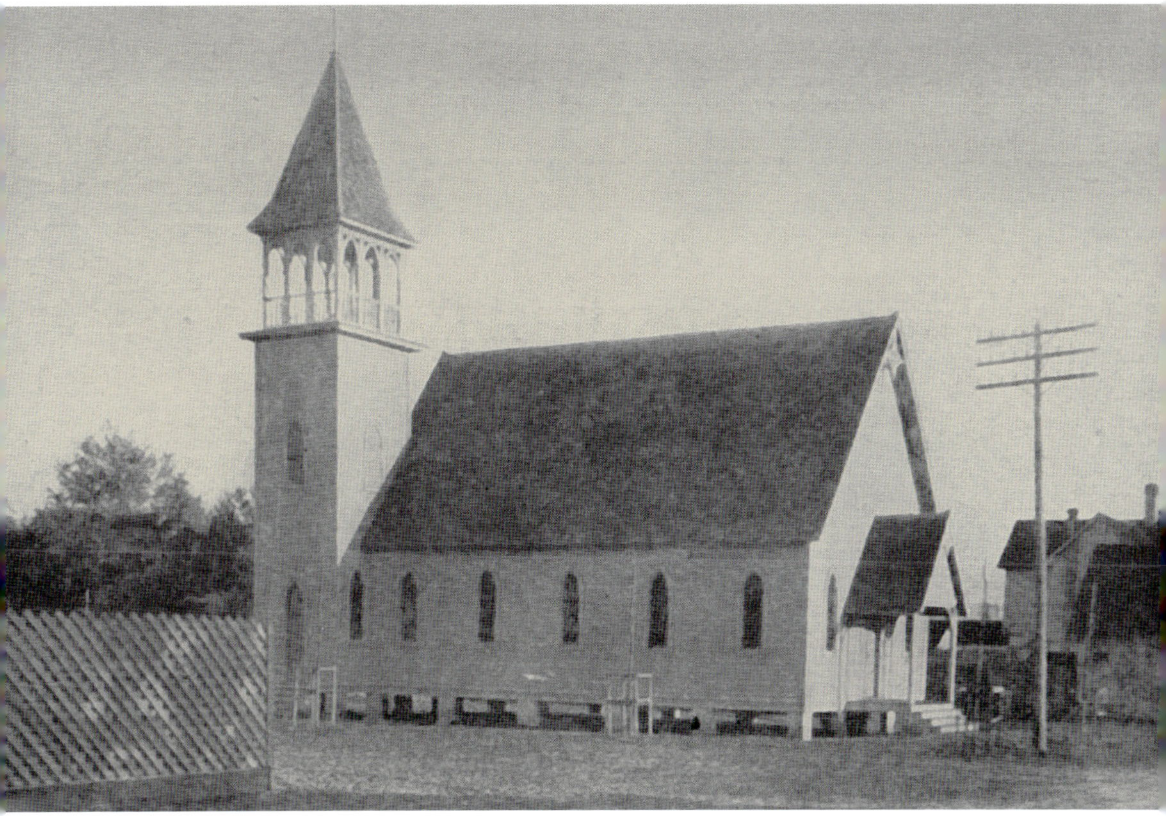

In 1889, the Episcopal Church purchased property on the southeast corner of Wheeler and Mahoney Streets for the purpose of building a parish. The Reverend J. H. Wardell, rector at Thonotosassa, rode horseback and conducted services for the local membership. Simple in design, the original building was moved to its present site at 302 Carey Street in the early 1950s and has undergone extensive remodeling and expansion.

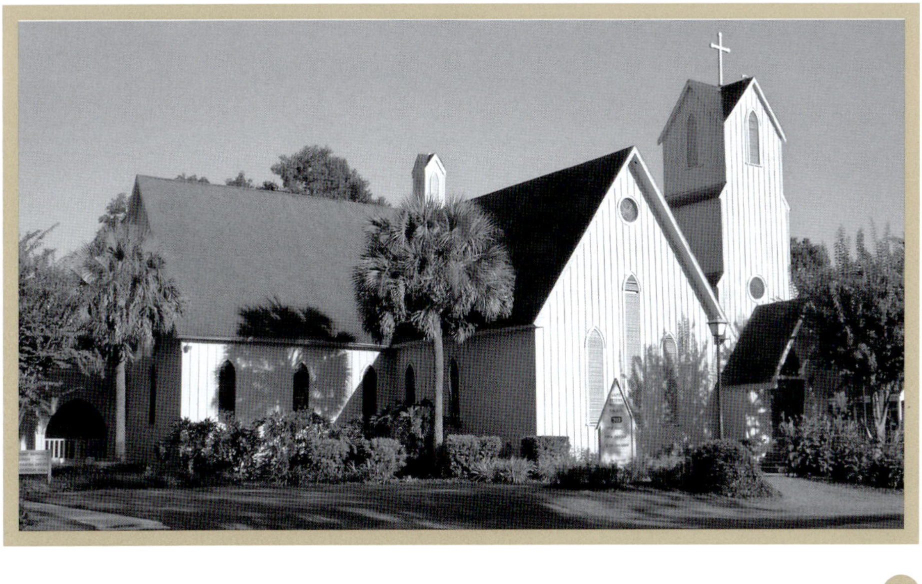

A 1913 postal card, a gift of Mrs. D. M. McKey, depicts the wooden structure that was built in 1902. Some of the stained-glass windows from this building were moved to and installed in the new church building when it was completed in 1926. The First United Methodist Church members recently celebrated their 125th Anniversary.

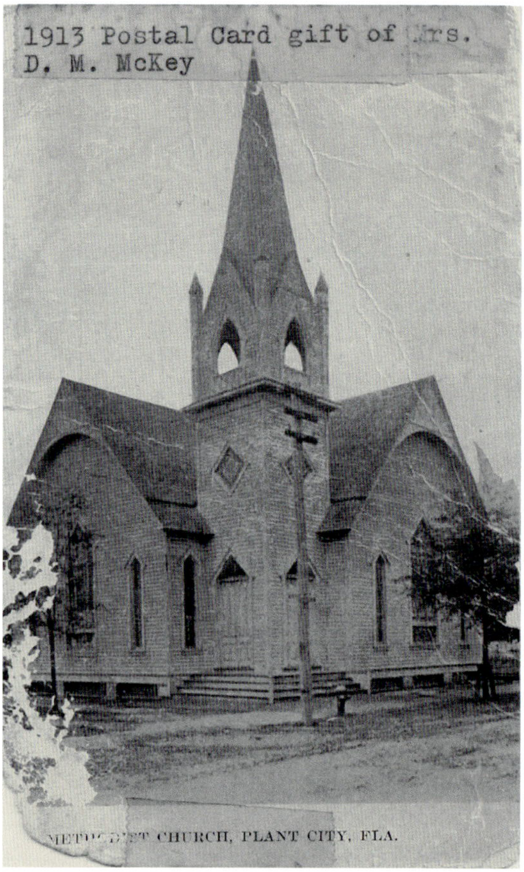

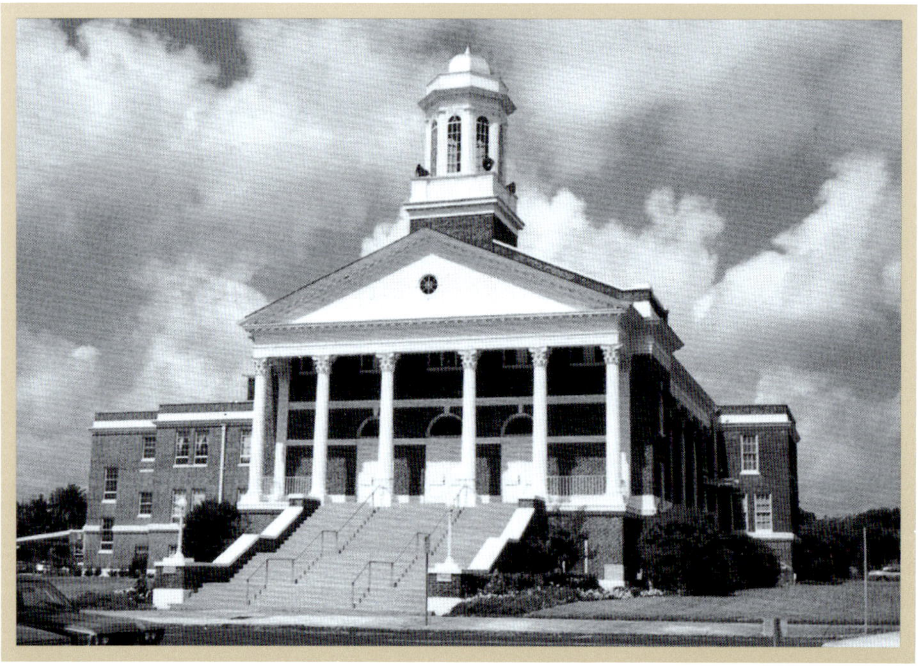

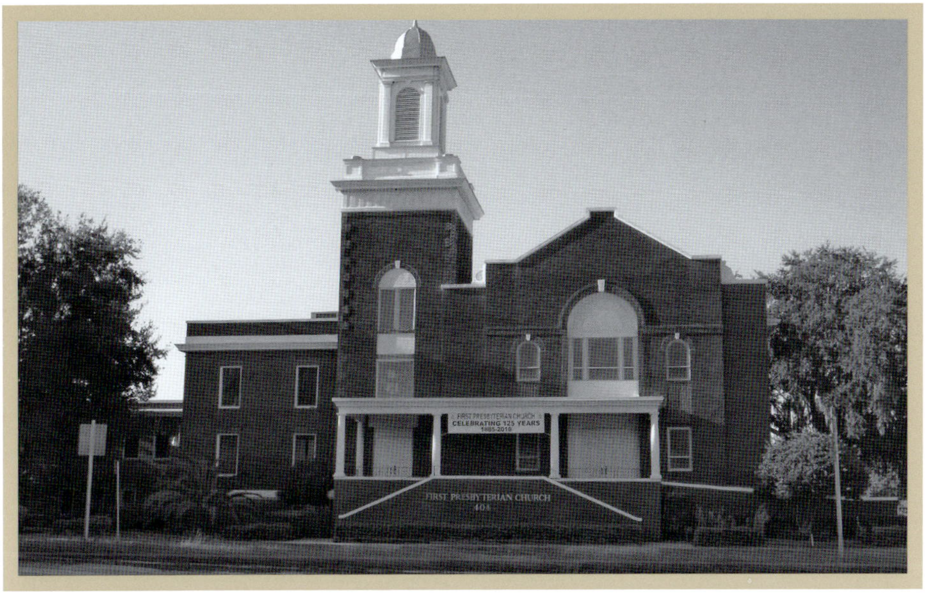

The current First Presbyterian Church was built on the same site in 1924 as the 1892 church. The front steps have been altered to accommodate a side-entry ramp, and a front portico has been added. The original member listing was of 19 people. The First Presbyterian Church Learning Center is an early childhood educational facility.

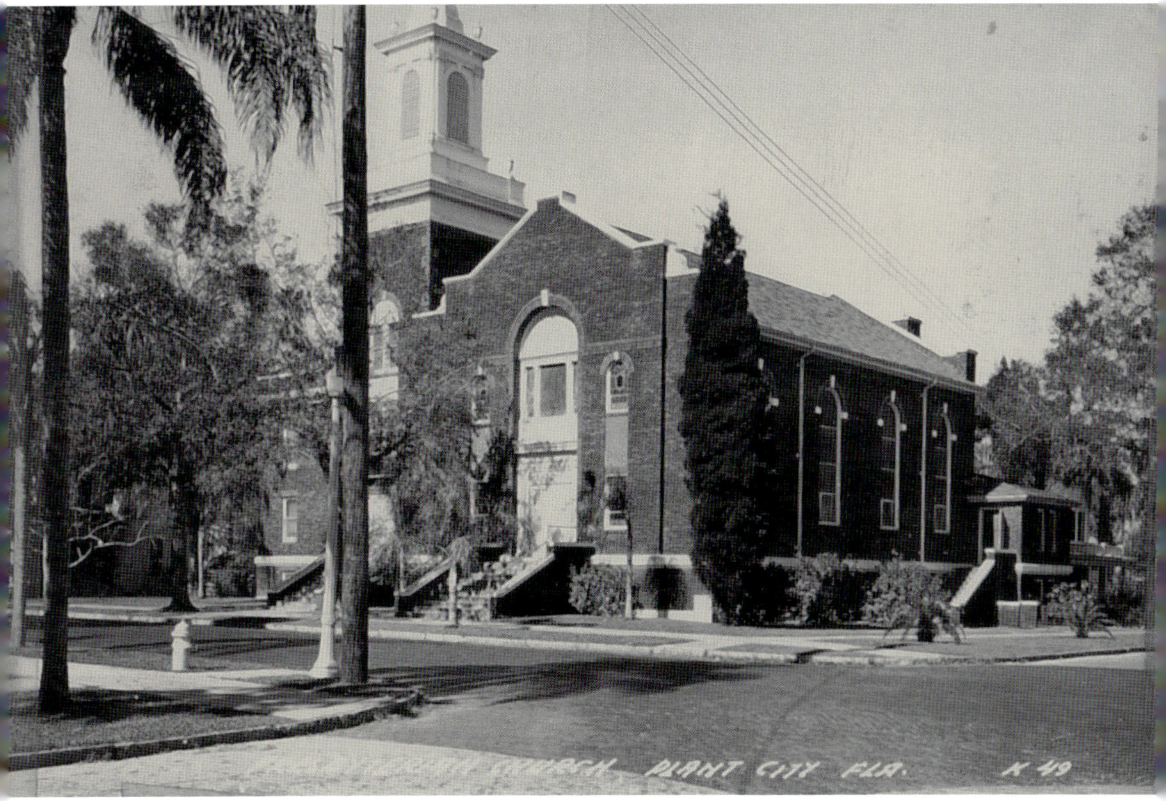

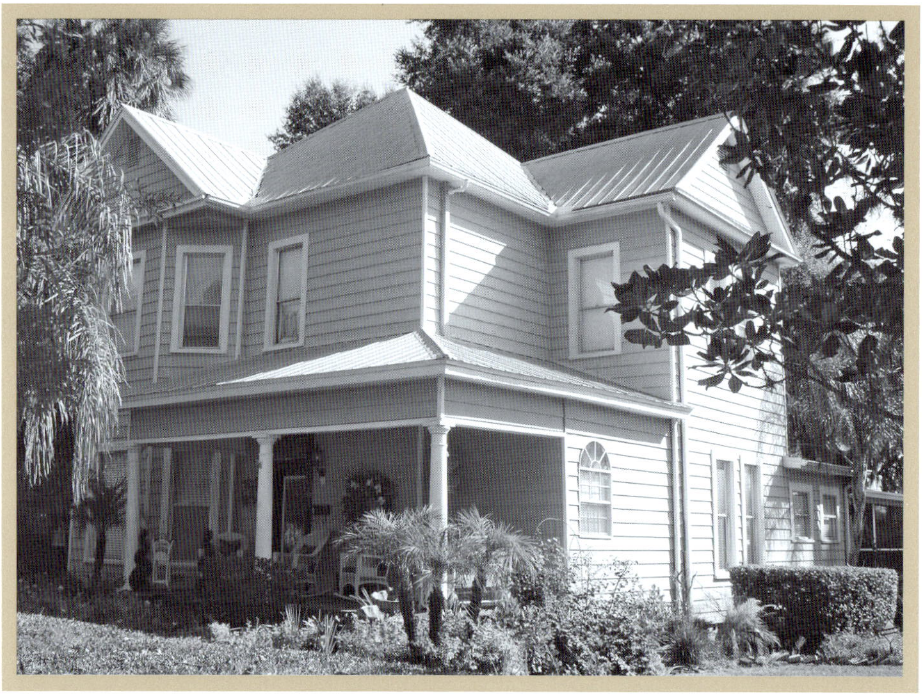

The First Presbyterian Church Manse, built in 1907, was moved from its Reynolds Street location to the northeast corner of Collins and Gilchrist Streets in 1961. The elegant two-story, 3,700-square-foot home includes eight rooms with bay windows on both the first and second floors. The wraparound porches seen on the early postcard did not survive the move. It is now a private residence.

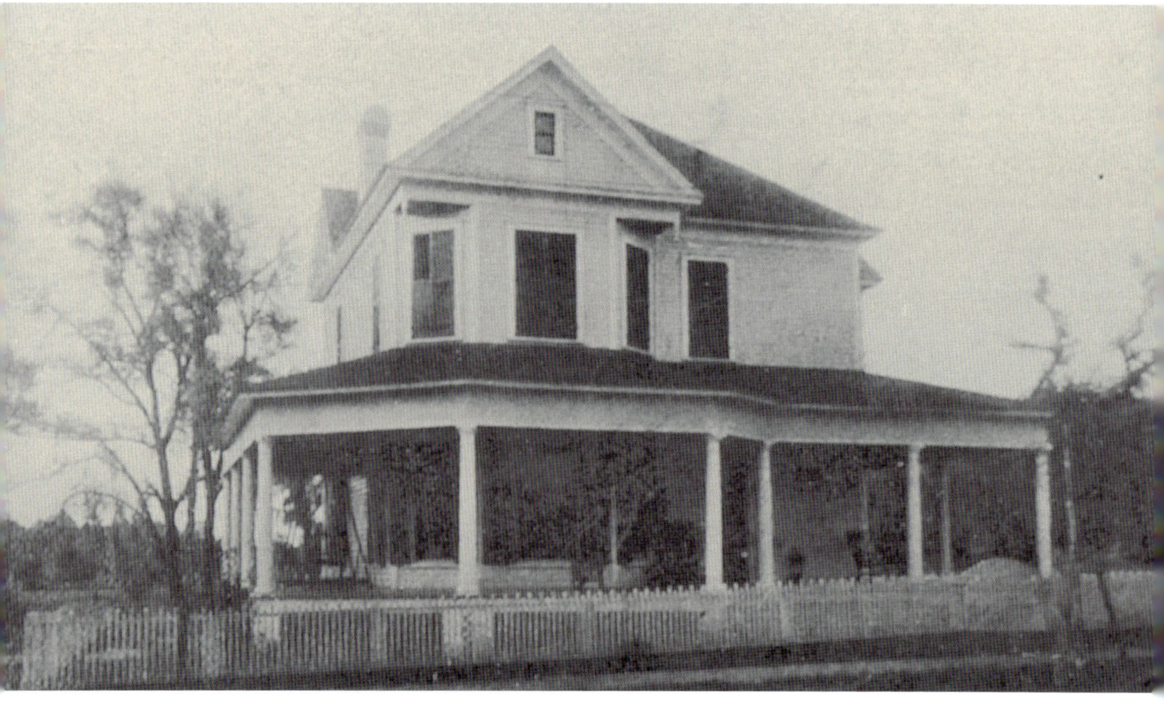

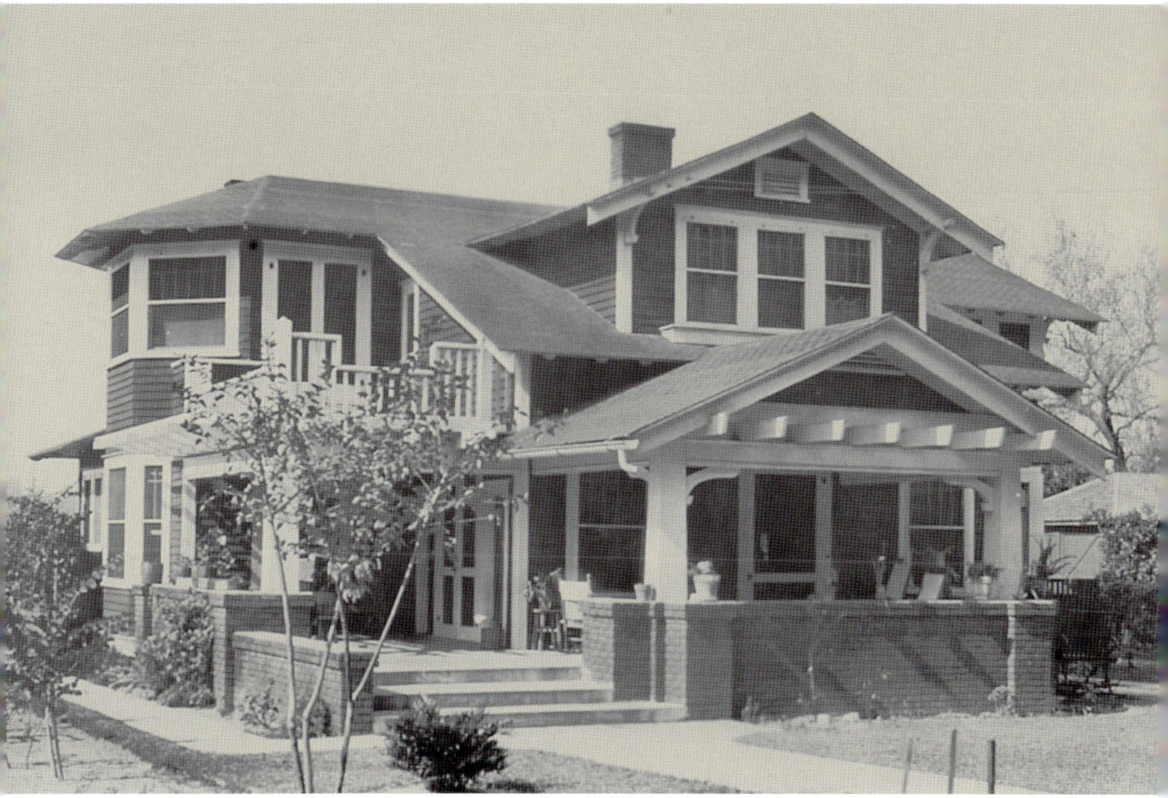

This craftsman-style bungalow of wood and brick was built in 1916 for Frank McGuire. In 1921, William A. House and his wife, May, moved to the home and lived there for quite a few years. The north side has a second story over the porte cochere. The home has maintained a generous portion of its original style. Damaged by an interior fire, the architectural elements of this home's exterior still contribute to the historical neighborhood. A 1990 architectural review noted that this house was the finest example of a bungalow-style residence in Plant City.

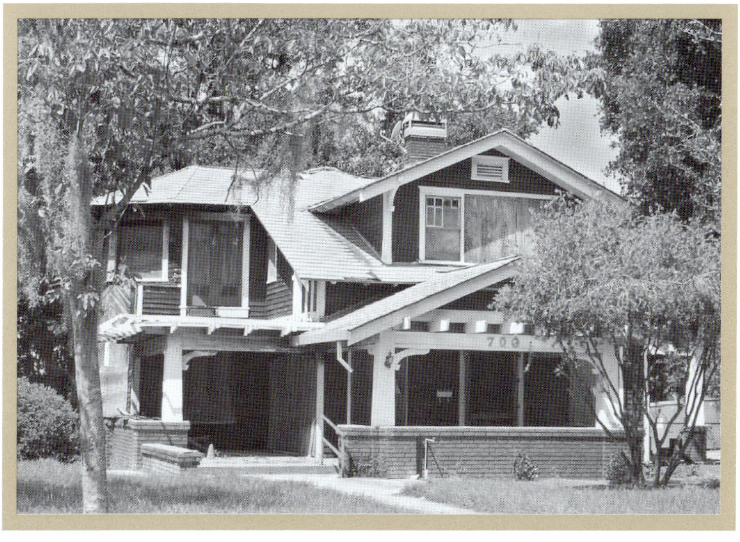

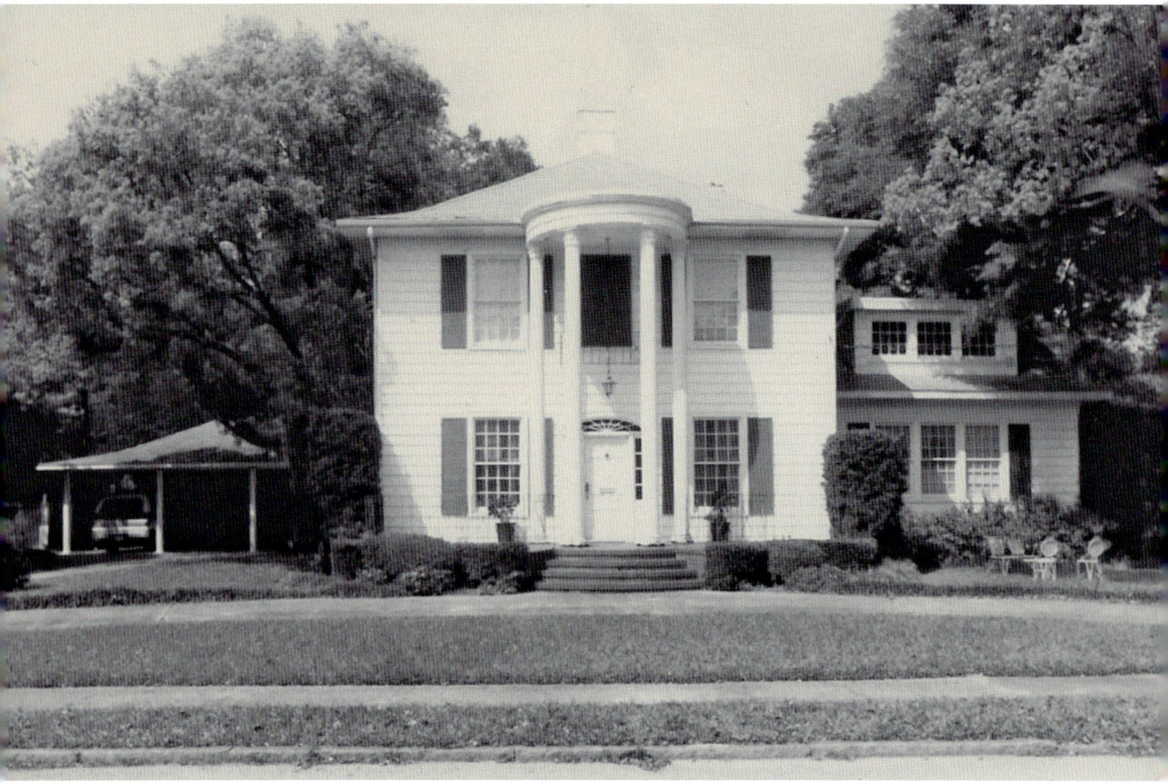

Built in 1912 of the Colonial Revival influence, this stately residence's 1960s remodel added the tall Corinthian columns that support the front entry. It features a symmetrical facade with 12 over 12 windows and a fan window above the door with sidelights, establishing a formal appearance. The semicircular portico and circular drive entryway are impressive. This home has always been a private residence.

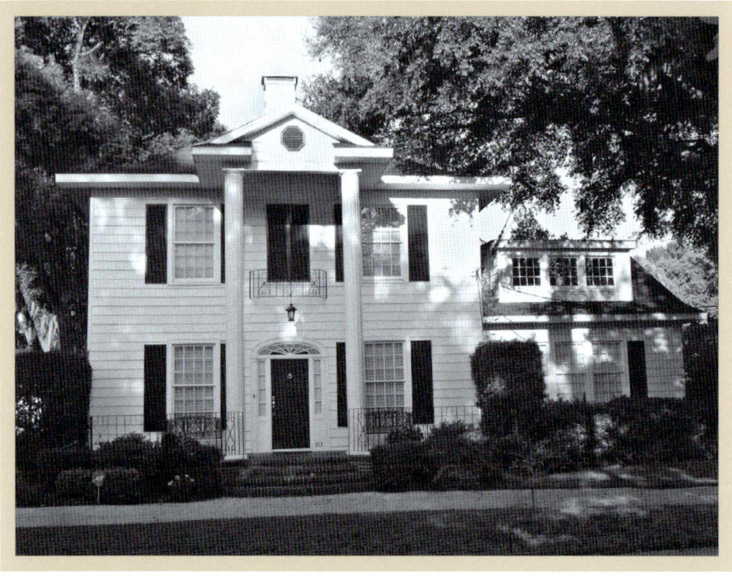

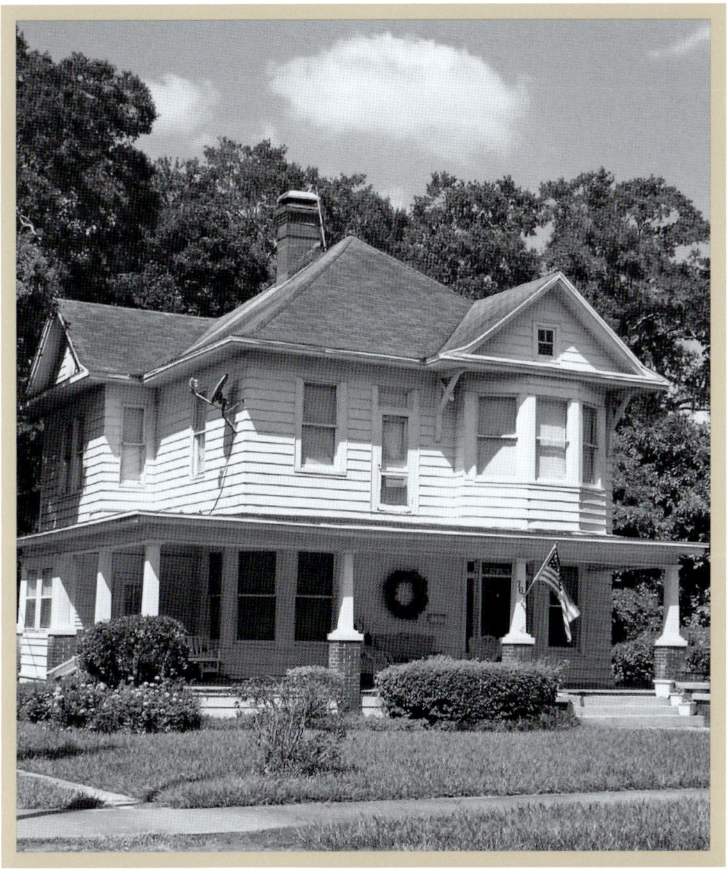

The residence of C. A. Root was built in 1910. The footprint of this Queen Anne–style home has remained as originally designed. The stone and wrought-iron fencing shown in the earlier postcard, along with the two widow's walk porches on the second story and the roof top widow's walk, have all been removed. Root, being involved in the timber business, only used the finest of building materials in the construction of this grand home.

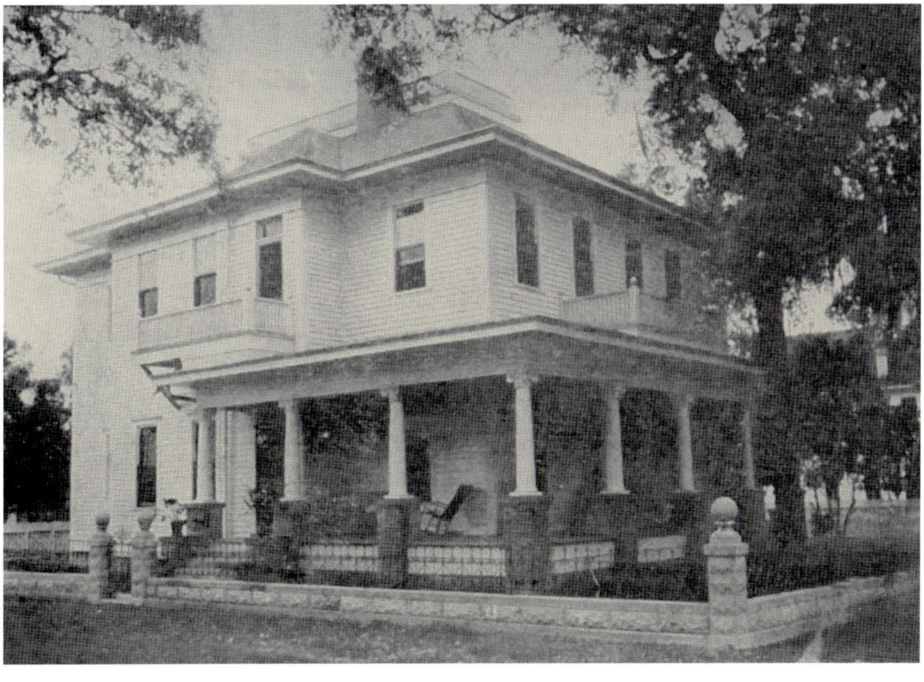

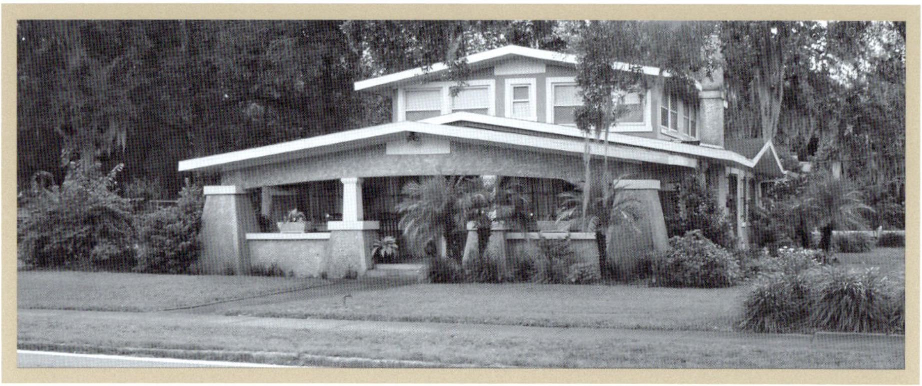

Mrs. Ivey Register's bungalow residence was built in 1922. This fine stucco home on North Wheeler Street cost $5,000. R. E. Lee of Tarpon Springs was the contractor. The decorative wire fence and low sidewalk curbing has long since been removed. The upstairs of the home was leased to renters. Now it exists as a private residence.

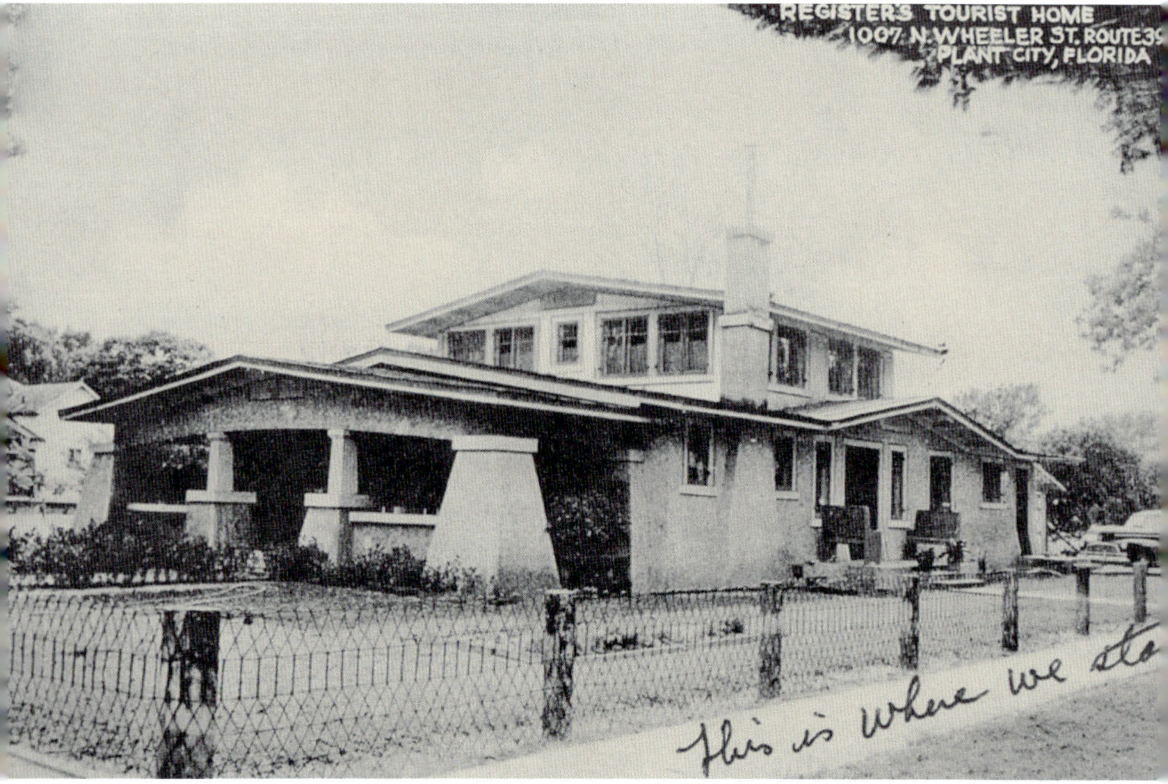

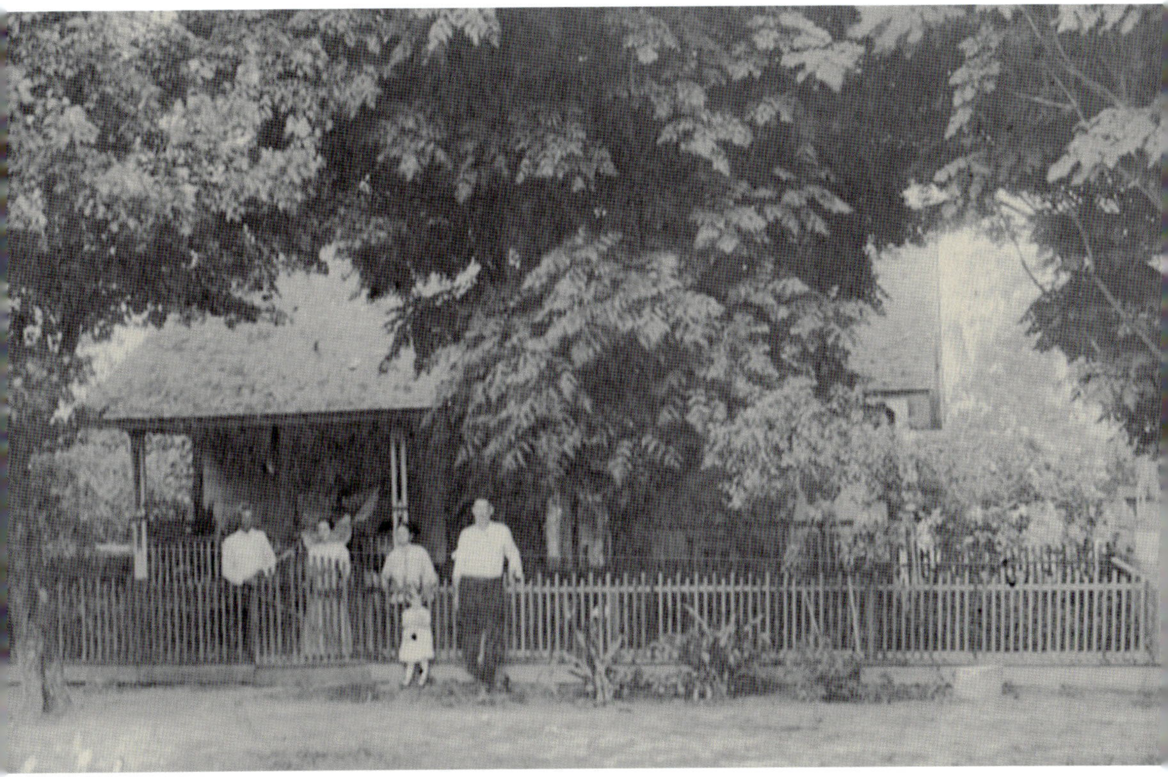

One of Plant City's early settlers, John S. Thomas, is seen in this early photograph (in front of the fence) at his Thonotosassa Road home with one of his sons (name unknown) and his daughters Lillian and Annie Mae Thomas Knott, as well as granddaughter Lillian Knott. For many years, Oakwood Trailer Park occupied this site. Now the busy site located at the corner of Thonotosassa Road and U.S. Highway 92 West is home to a 24-hour Walgreens.

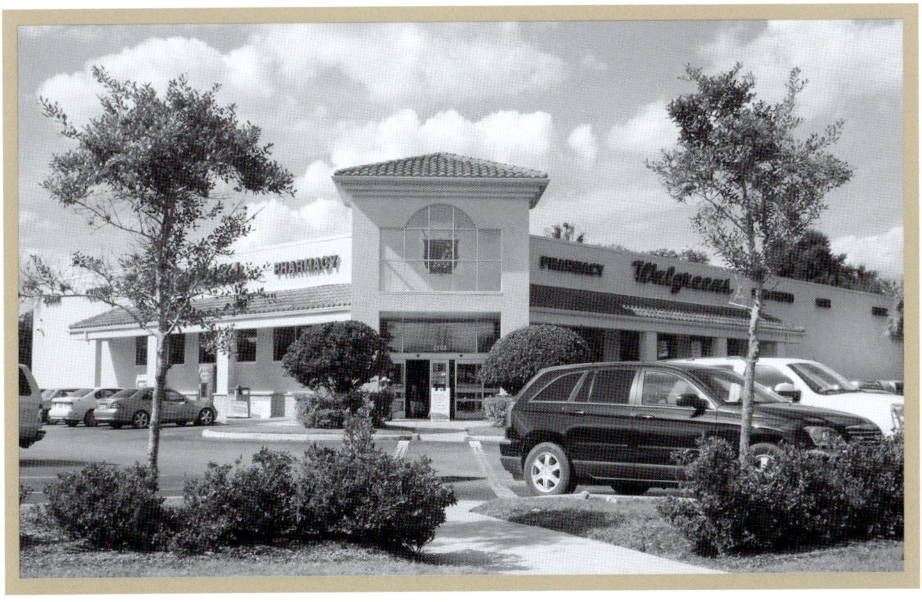

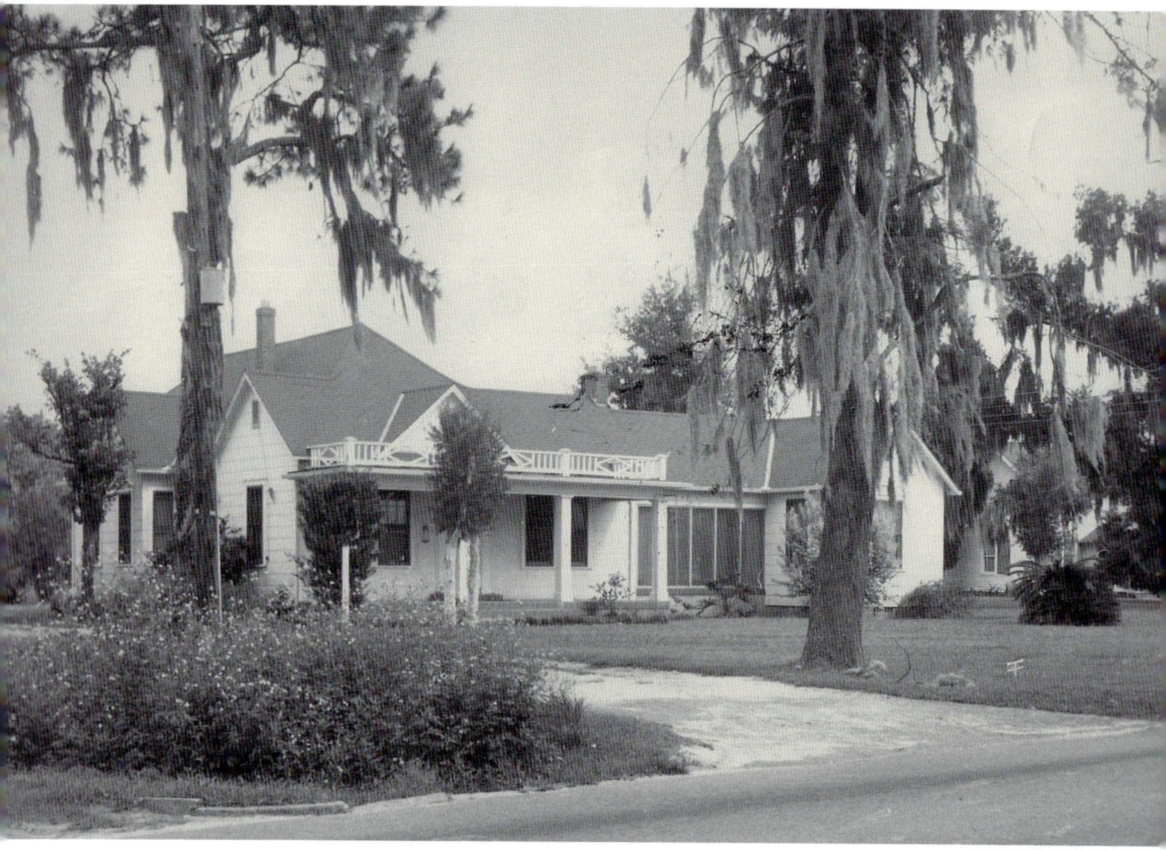

The ranch-style single-story home of Dwight L. and Mary G. Crum on the Collins Street extension (beyond city limits) has a similar style of a house located on West Calhoun Street. Crum was involved in the cattle industry, and his family resided in this home until recently. Currently it is the location for the Cottages, an antique shop that also offers art lessons.

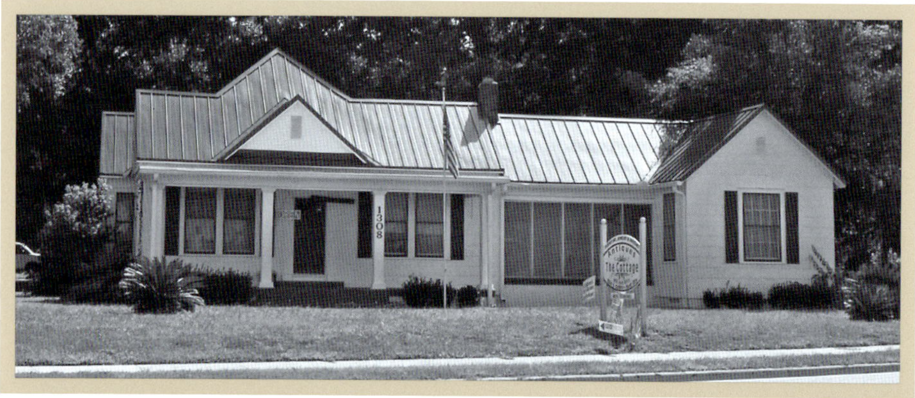

CHAPTER 5

FAMILY AND SOCIAL LIFE

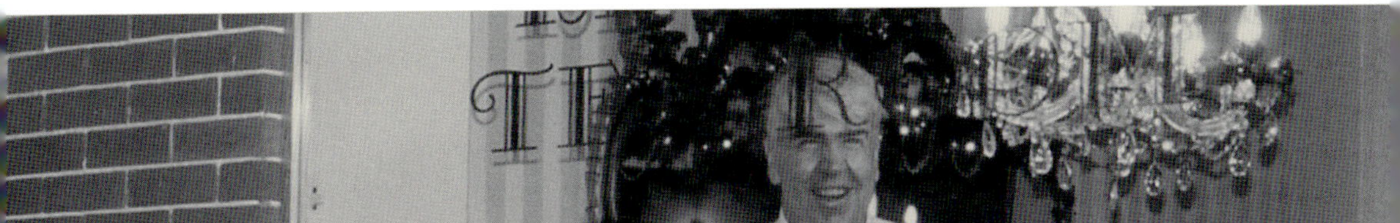

The Orange Blossom Tea Room was opened on December 1, 1994, by restaurateur Jim Pollard. Offering a full-service restaurant and catering facility, many local social events were enjoyed here in this historical building of 1910. Pollard designed and baked the replica cake of the 1914 Plant City High School as seen on page 46 of this book. He retired in 2009.

Charlotte Rosenberg was crowned queen of East Hillsborough's first annual strawberry festival at the opening ceremonies on March 12, 1930. The daughter of Sam and Fannie Rosenberg, she was a member of the senior class at Plant City High School. The 2010 Florida Strawberry Festival® queen, Natalie Burgin, is a high school junior with college plans to study international affairs. She is the daughter of Tom and Ricky Burgin.

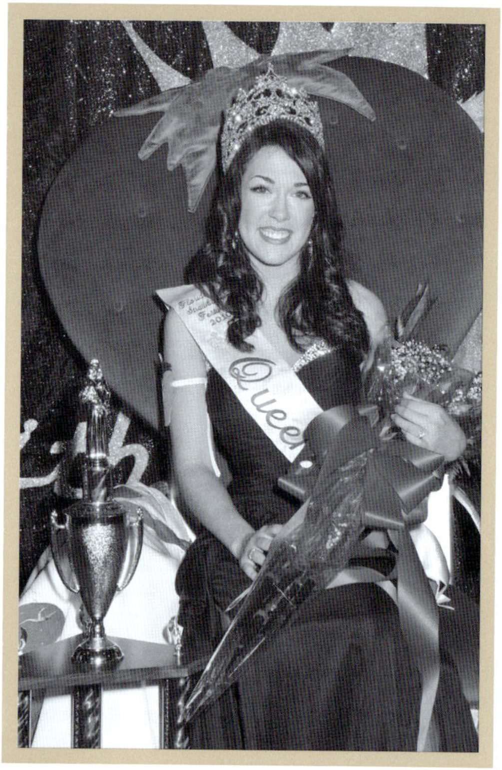

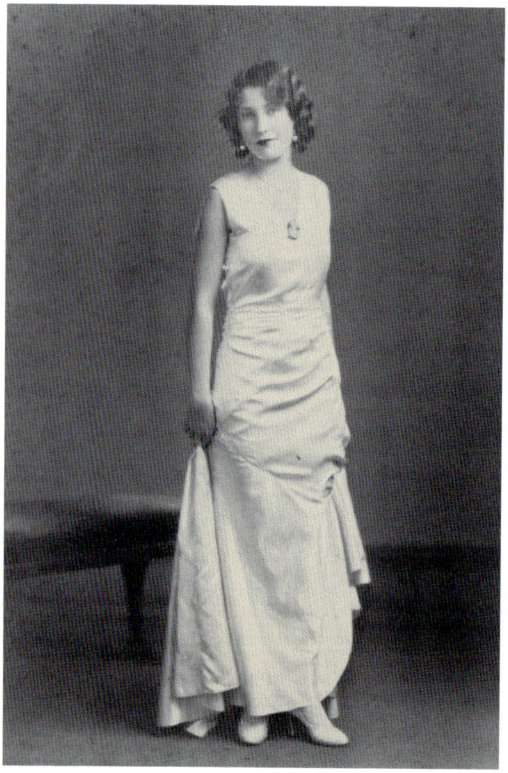

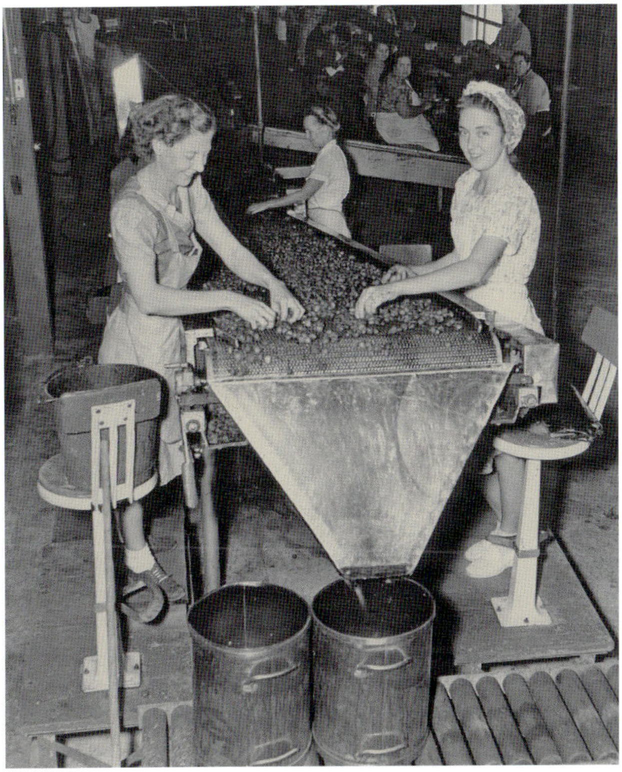

The women of the community have always selected the best of the strawberries. The earlier photograph shows two workers carefully selecting berries at Processing Shed No. 4 at the farmer's market in Plant City. In the 2010 photograph, Aleen Meyer, an East Hillsborough Historical Society volunteer, is stemming fresh strawberries. The berries are used for the society's shortcake booth at the festival.

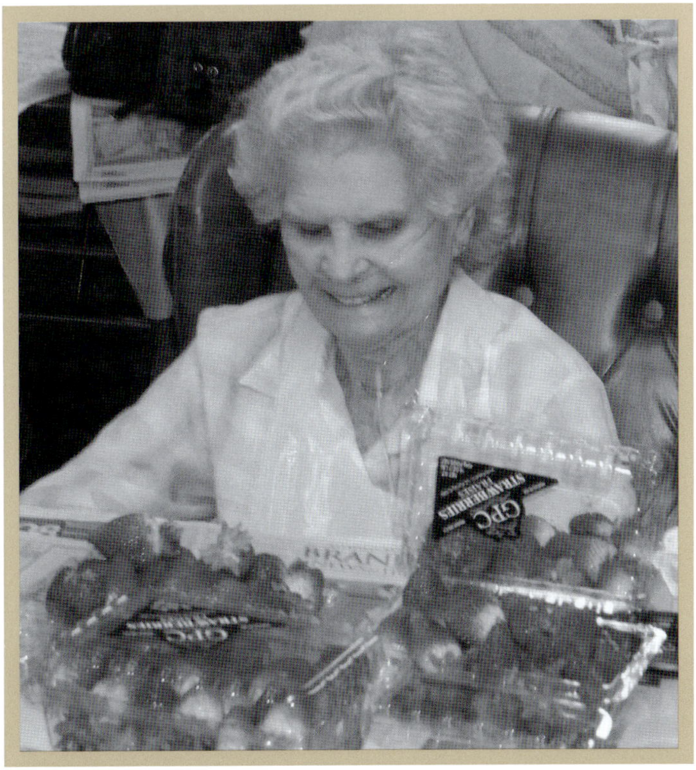

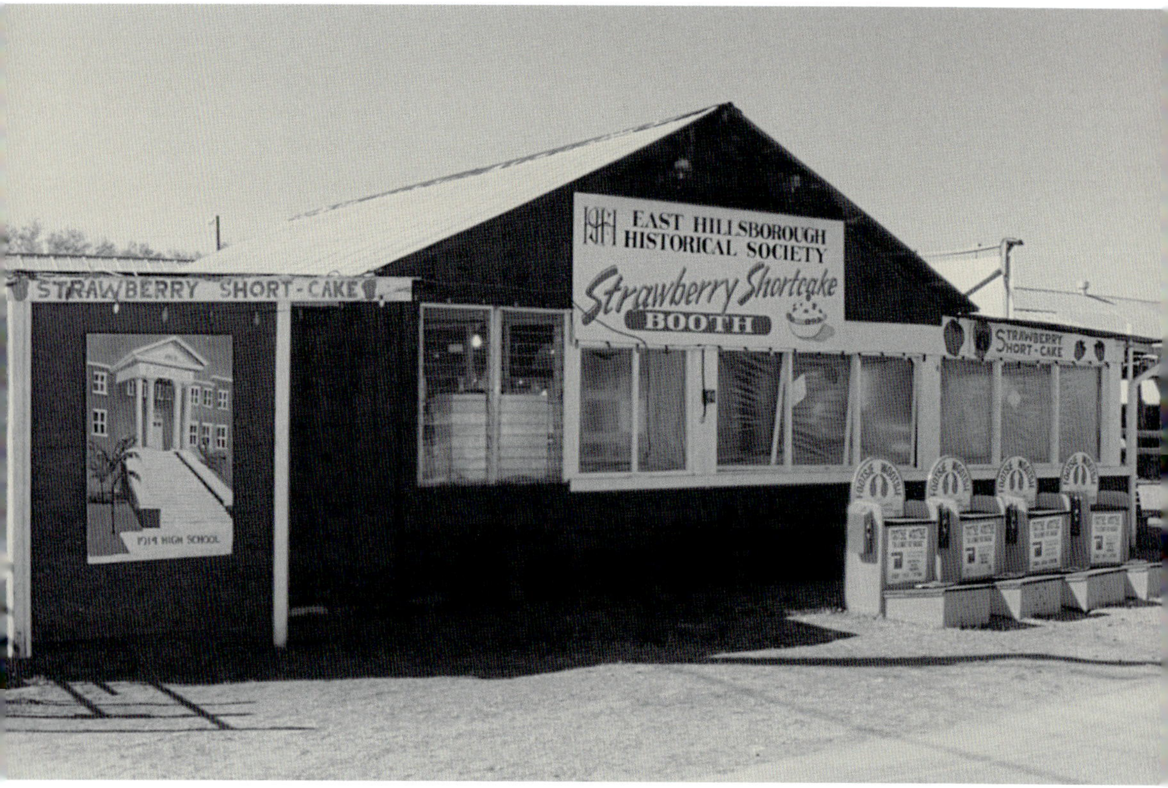

The East Hillsborough Historical Society's strawberry shortcake booth at the annual Florida Strawberry Festival® is the main fund-raiser and source of income for the society. The 11-day event requires hundreds of hours of volunteer service. The booth is located in the Pioneer Village area of the festival grounds. Whether Biscuit or cake, fresh berries and whipped cream are all that the recipe calls for.

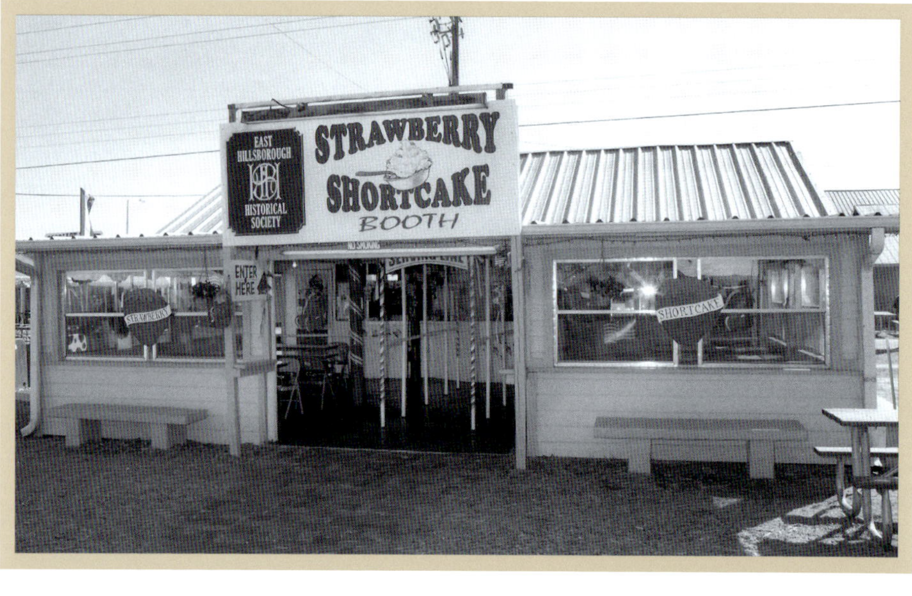

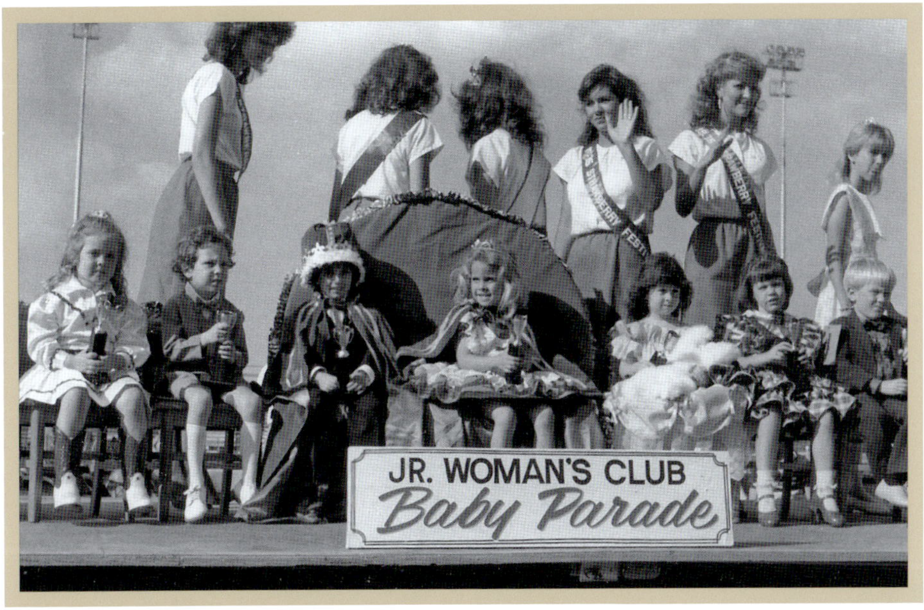

Part of the 11-day celebration of the annual Florida Strawberry Festival® is the popular contests and pageants. A 1936 Baby Parade contestant was James C. McCall. He is ready for the march in front of the judges' panel. Pictured standing, from left to right, are T. J. McCall, his son James, officer John Kirkland, and police chief J. A. Abbott. The 1975 Baby Parade queen, king, and court are on stage with their trophies, receiving gratulatory wishes from the reigning Florida Strawberry Festival® queen and court.

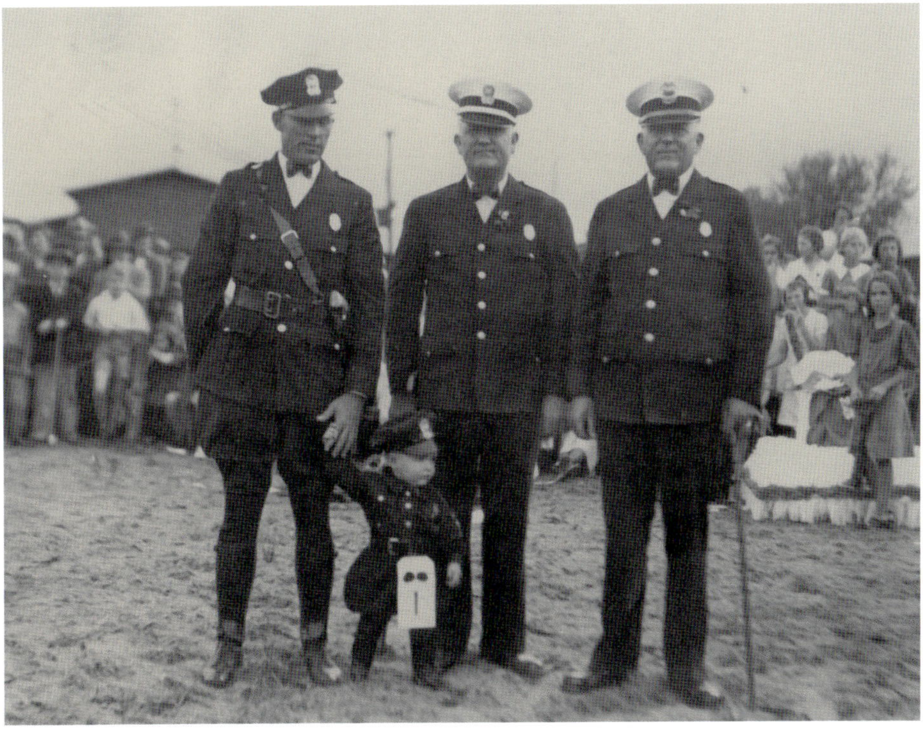

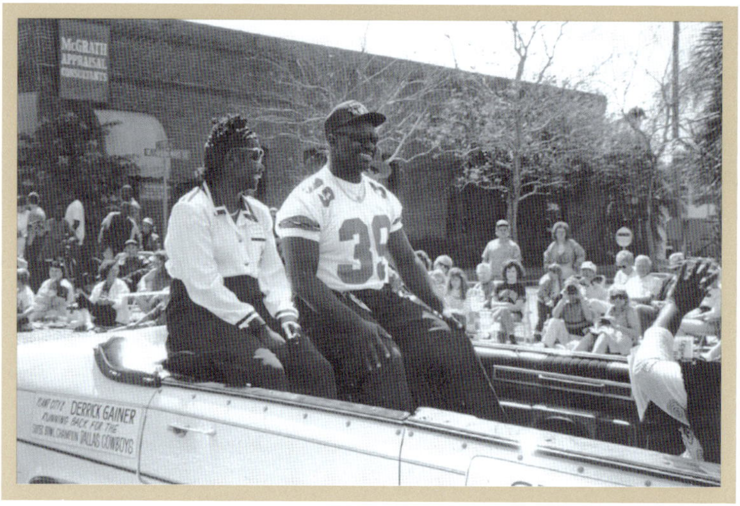

Spectators lined up along Haines Street to watch the annual parade. Floats were pulled by jeeps, trucks, and cars representing businesses, civic organizations, and officials. The street name was changed to Dr. Martin Luther King Jr. Boulevard to honor the late civil rights leader. Plant City native Derrick Gainer, a running back for the Super Bowl–winning Dallas Cowboys, came home and was the grand marshal for the annual Florida Strawberry Festival® Parade.

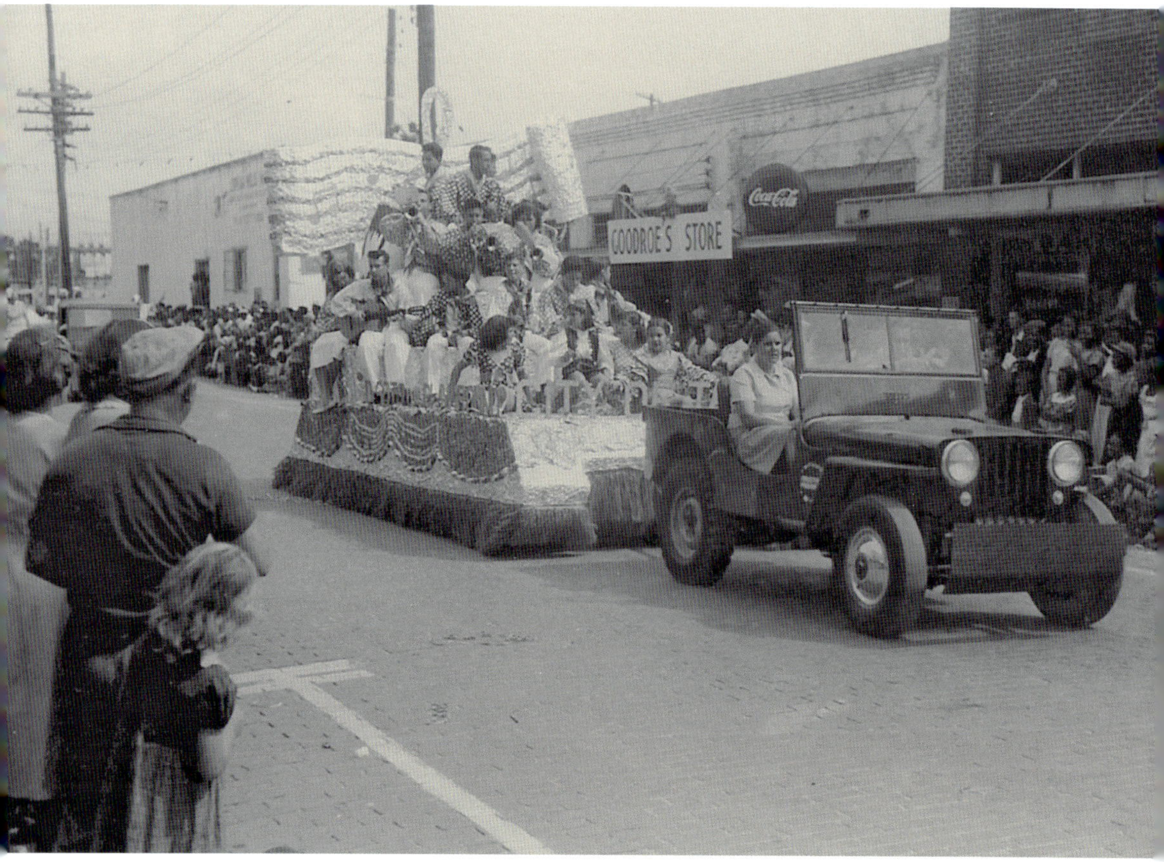

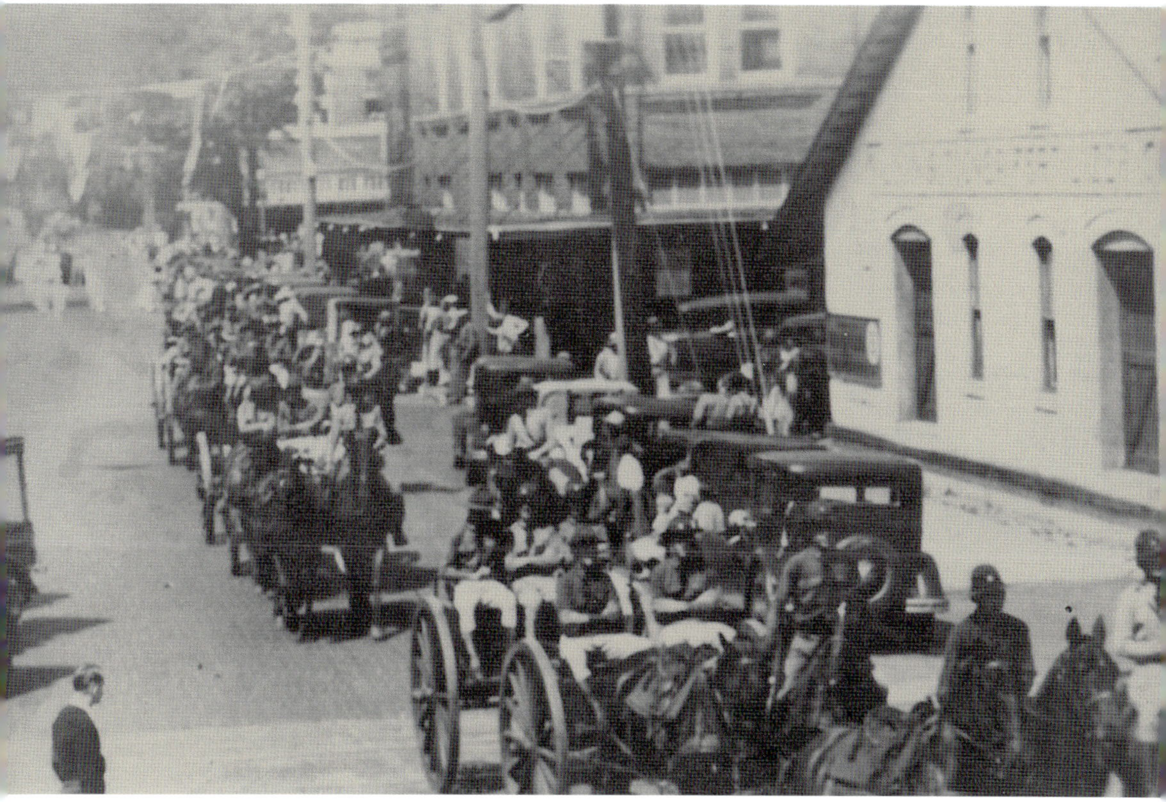

Parade goers are lined up along South Evers Street to watch the Annual Florida Strawberry Festival® Parade in 1932. Participants rode in horse-drawn wagons. More current parades feature platform floats that are driven or pulled. T. G. Robinson Jr., whose family owned the Robinson Pool and Skating Rink, is driving his 1946 Ford with a float full of beauties. The lady on top of the skate is his wife, Laverne Herring Robinson. The pool and skating rink was a popular recreational place for everyone.

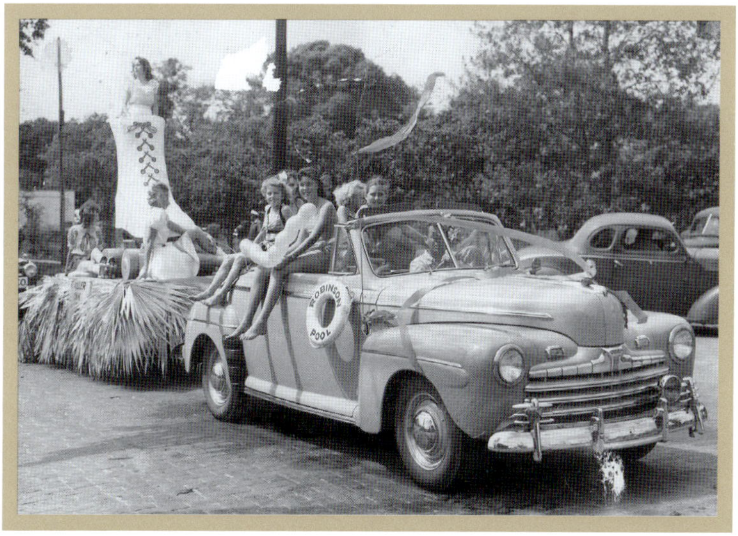

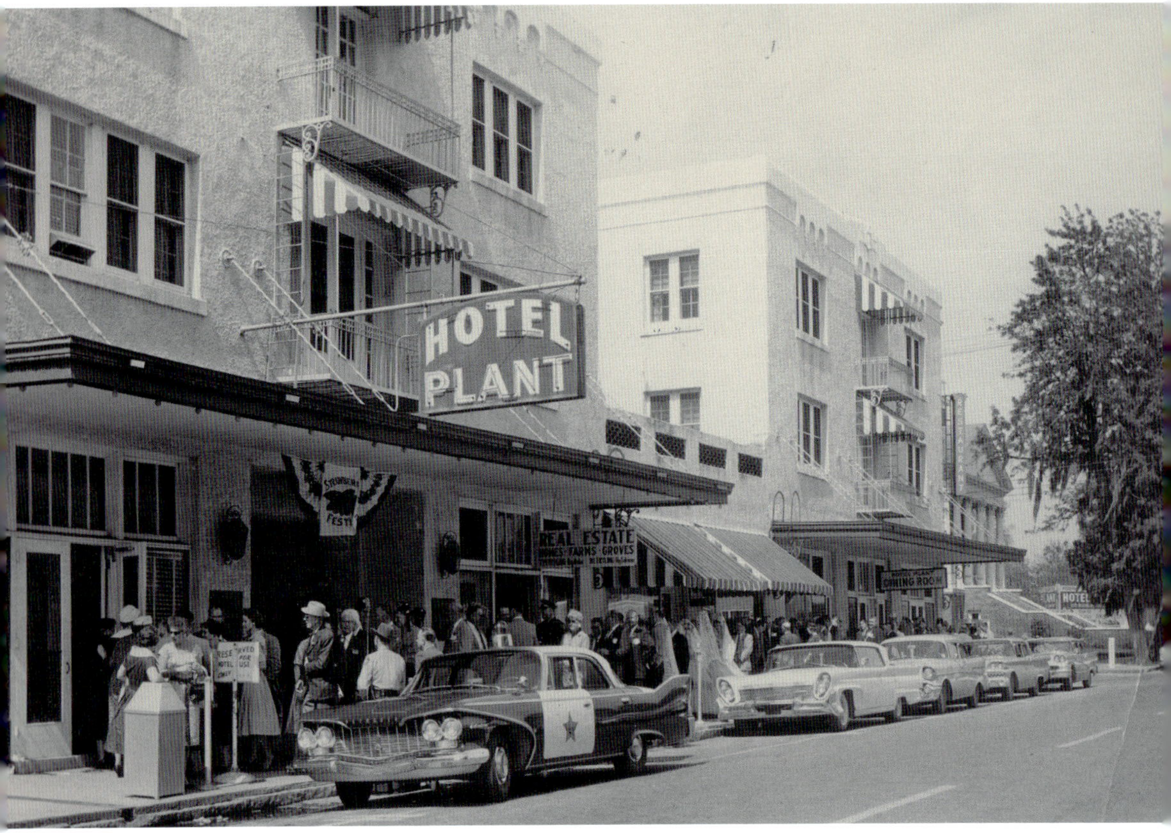

The Hotel Plant was the site of the annual kickoff luncheon for the festival. Officials, dignitaries, and invited guests attended the luncheon prior to the start of the parade. Years later, the luncheon moved to the front lawn of the Tampa Electric Company offices on West Haines Street. Drawing a bigger crowd every year, the luncheon is now held at the John R. Trinkle Center on the Plant City campus of Hillsborough Community College. Parade grand marshals, mother and daughter singing duo Naomi and Wynonna Judd, are being driven in a Corsair convertible. The Corsair was custom made by the driver, Tobe Anna Robinson and the late Ken Fleming.

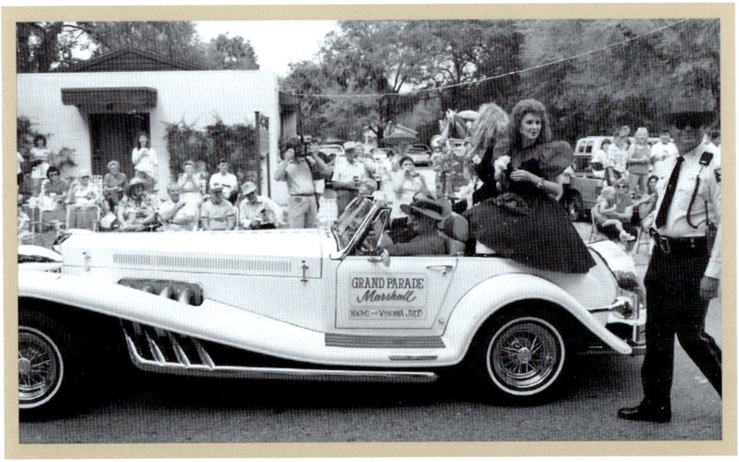

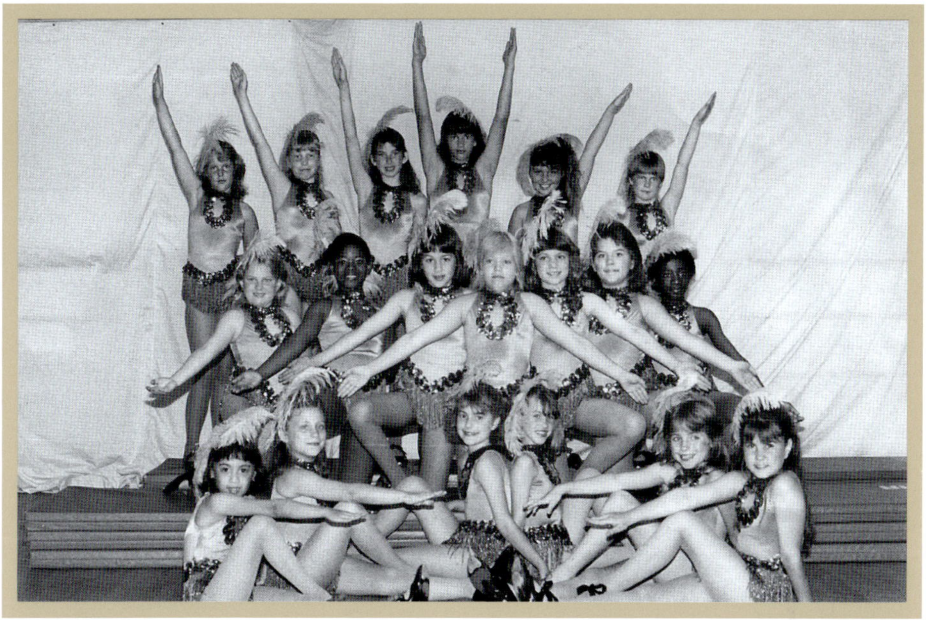

Some of Plant City's finest ladies kick up their heels with a little of the can-can. The fabulous home-talent production of *Follies of '49* was presented by the Woman's Club's welfare department. And just to prove that history can repeat itself, this adorable group of dancers from Jackie's Dance Theater put on a showstopping performance with their version of the can-can.

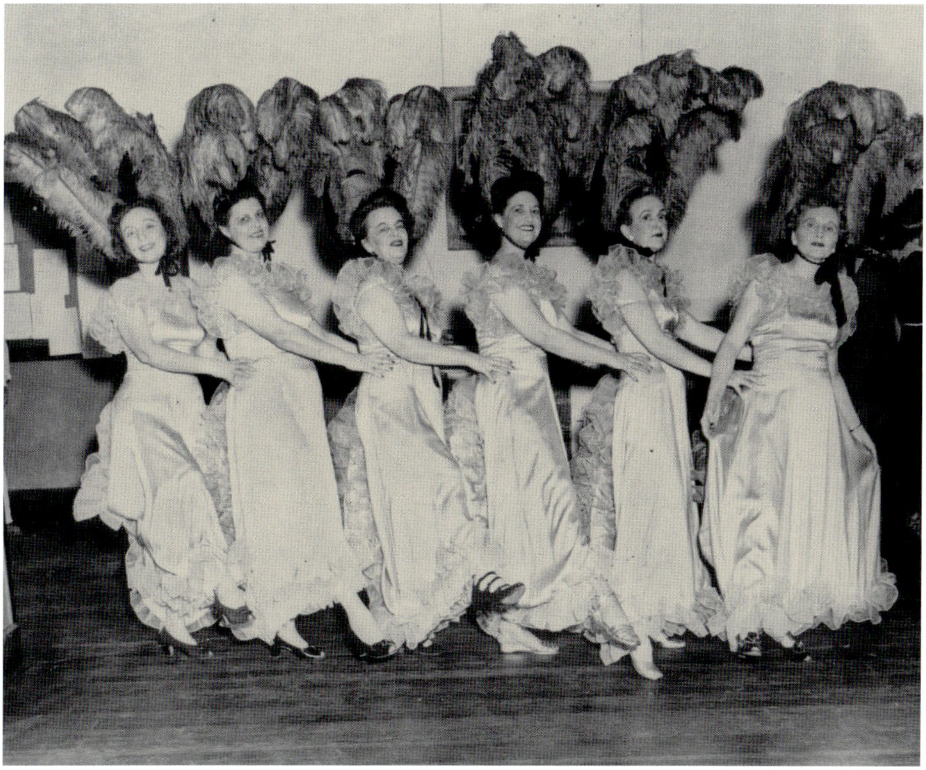

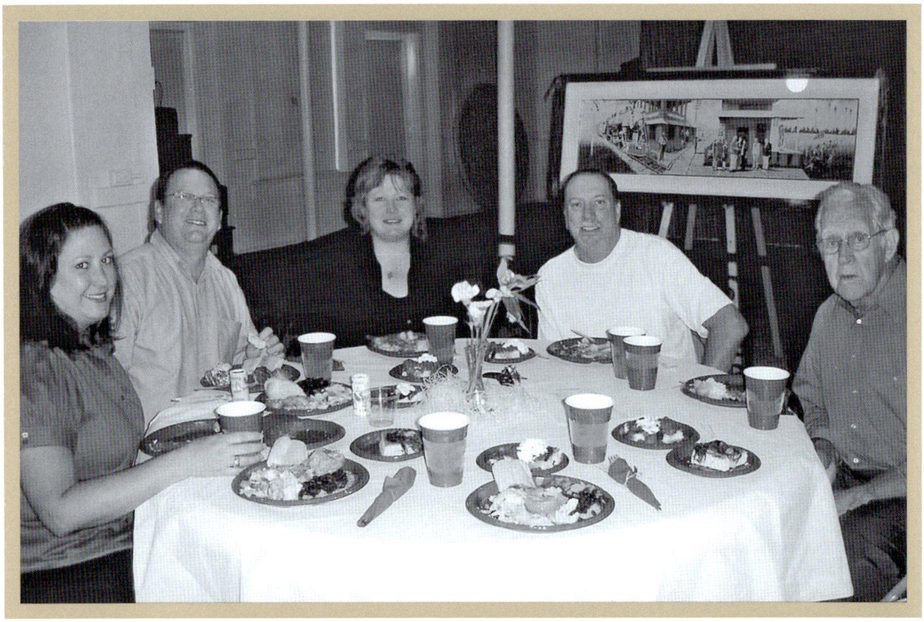

Gathered at the annual banquet for the East Hillsborough Historical Society in 1976, the newly installed members of the board of directors stood ready to take on their mission of "Preserving the Past for the Future." In the 2008 photograph at a dinner for the society are board members, from left to right, Marlene Haney Sanchez, Jose T. Sanchez III, Doresa Young, Pat Young, and Roy Wise.

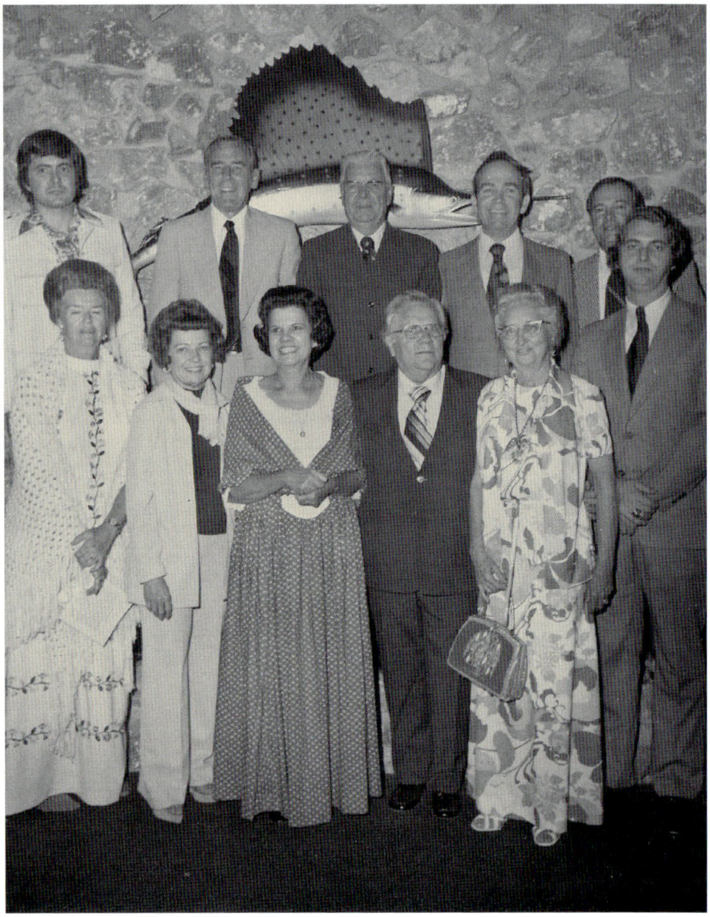

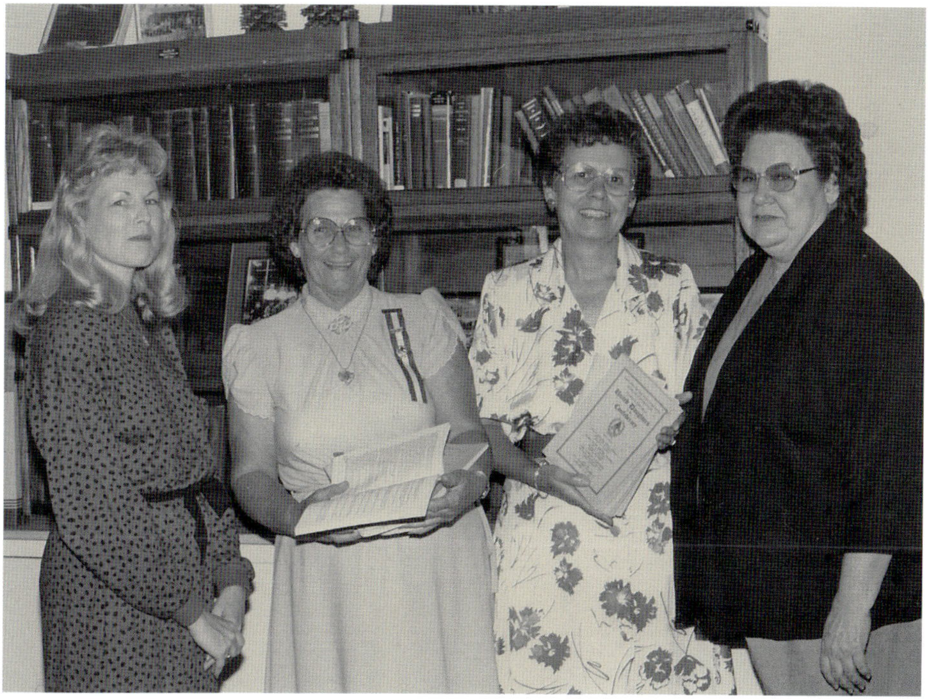

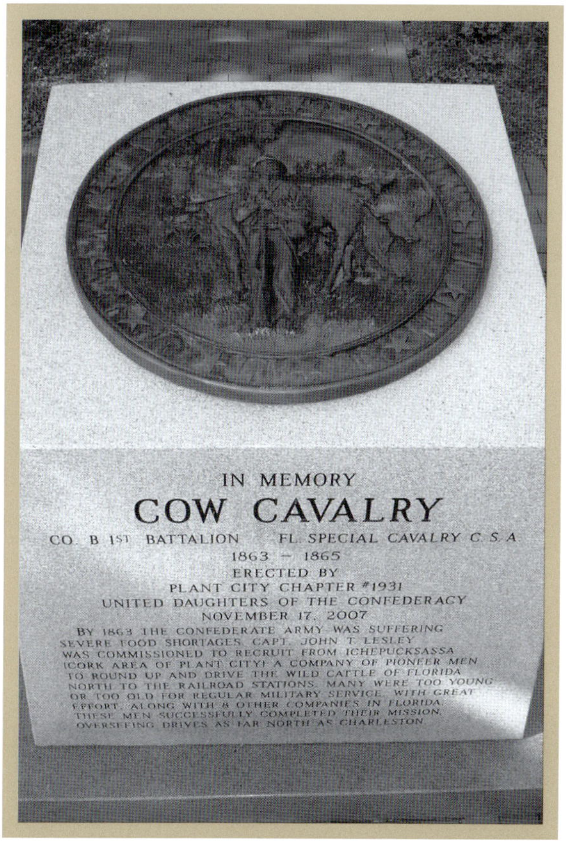

The Plant City chapter no. 1931 of the United Daughters of the Confederacy presented donations of publications of the minutes of the annual conventions of the Florida Division of UDC. The documents are an integral part of the collection of the Quintilla Geer Bruton Archives Center of the East Hillsborough Historical Society. Pictured from left to right are Shelby Bender, cochairman of the Archives Center; Alice B. Sikes and Diana Shuman, UDC members; and Mary Lee Barnes Harrell, cochairman of the Archives Center. The chapter continues to support the preservation of Plant City's community history. On November 17, 2007, at the Annual Pioneer Heritage Day celebration, a granite and bronze marker was dedicated in memory of the Cow Cavalry Company B 1st Battalion Florida Special Cavalry, CSA. Many of the members of this unit were from the eastern Hillsborough County community.

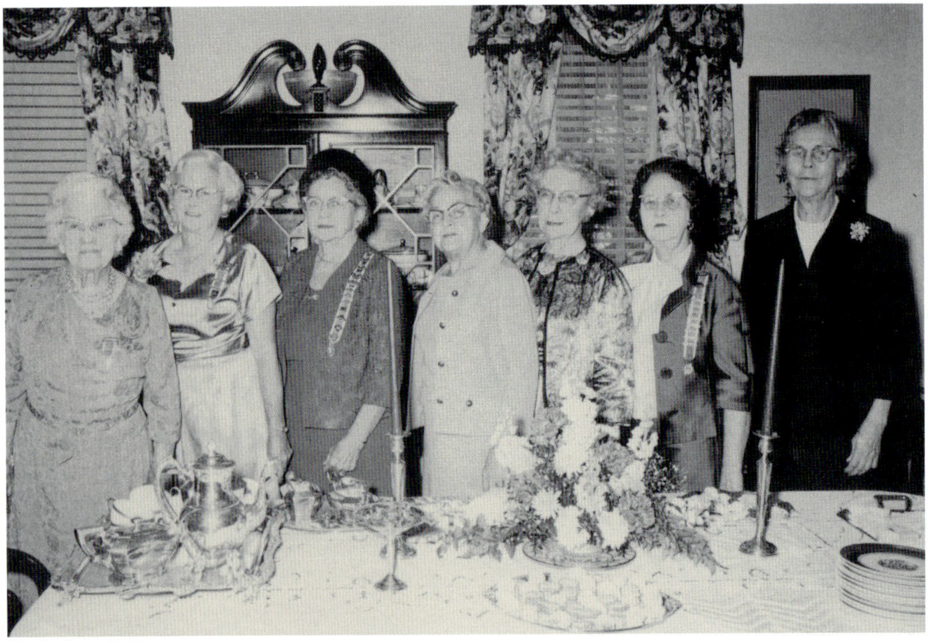

The Daughters of the American Revolution, Echebucasassa chapter, celebrated its 25th anniversary with tea at the home of Annie Schneider. Pictured from left to right are Annie Schneider, Euridice Simmons, Olga Davis, Annie Eberhardt, Alice E. Warner, Bessie Lamar Calvert, and Wilmoth Herron. Congratulating the chapter on its 75th anniversary celebration in 2004 in the picture below are, from left to right, State Regent Jean Dixon Mann, Sarah "Sally" Josephine Newsome Miller, and Margie Ruth Leverich Repole.

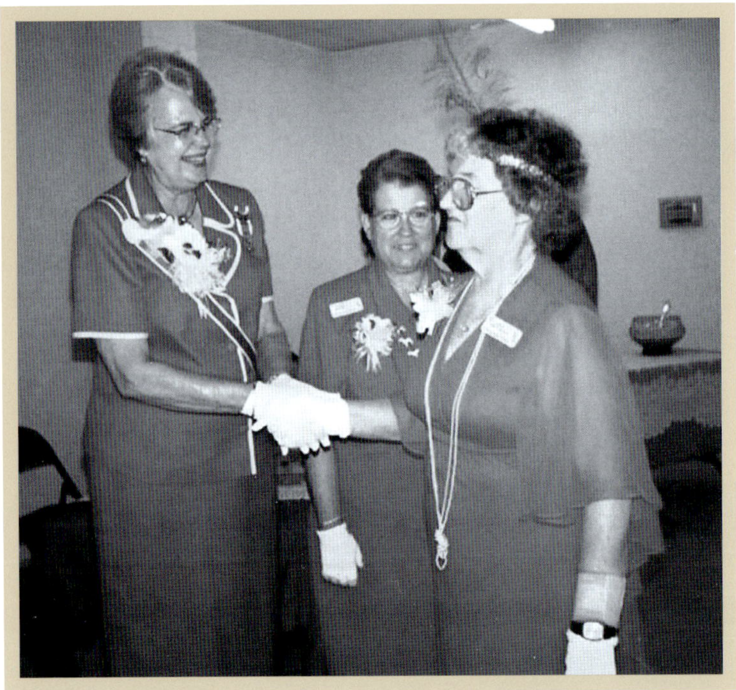

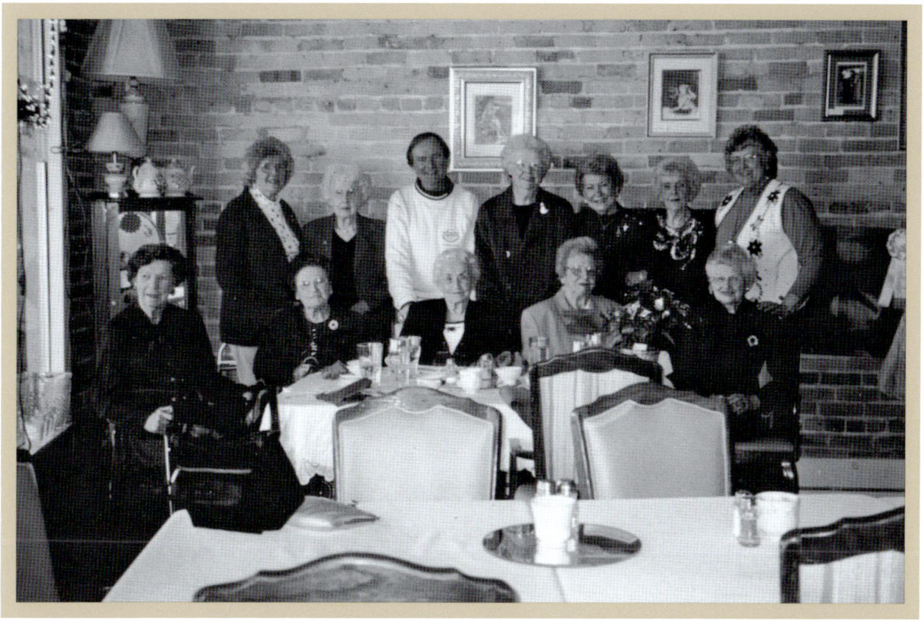

The First United Methodist Church of Plant City's Mary and Martha Sunday School class of 1950 is seen gathered for the annual ladies luncheon. The class had 37 members who acted as faithful servants to their church. In this 2002 photograph, the surviving members pose with Pastor Alan Beaver. From left to right are (sitting) Floda Cameron, Alice Williams, Willie Belle Doyell, Roberta Manley, and LaVon Cox; (standing) Vivian Dekle, Alma Comer, Reverend Beaver, Nancy Rollyson, Bette Heydrick, Arelette Fitzgibbons, and Miria Hester.

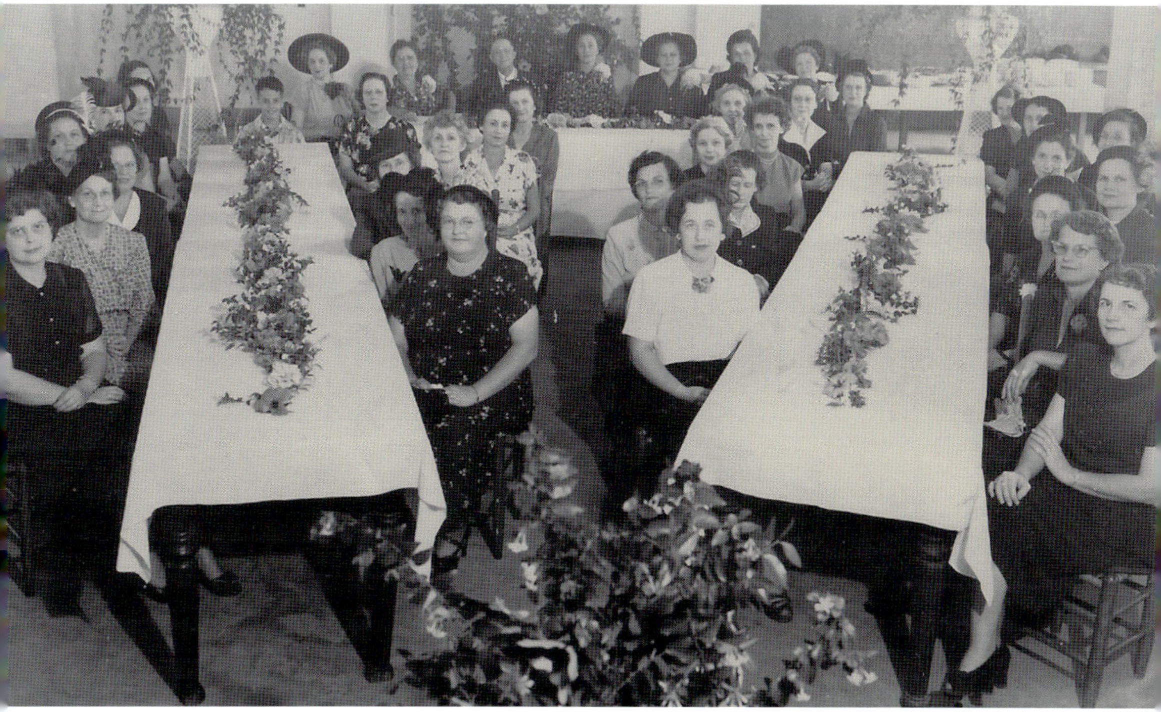

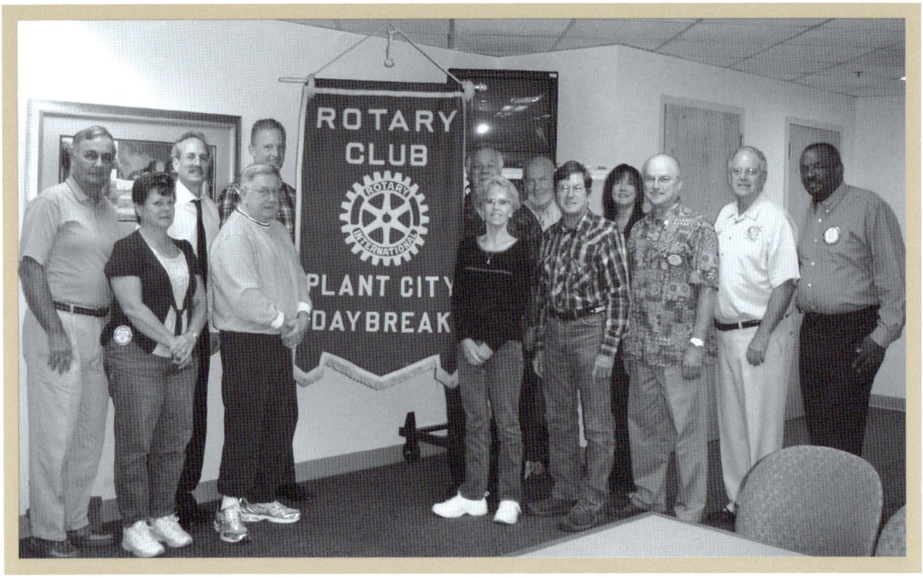

Plant City's service club organizations have always been active in participating in community events. In 1940, the Plant City Kiwanis Club member delegates attended the state convention in Jacksonville. Organized in 1921, the Kiwanis Club was Plant City's first men's civic club. Members included the town's prominent businessmen. In this 2010 photograph, members of the Rotary Club of Plant City Daybreak attend their weekly morning meeting in preparation to distribute dictionaries to the local elementary schools. The Rotary Club of Plant City Daybreak was one of the first local clubs with female members.

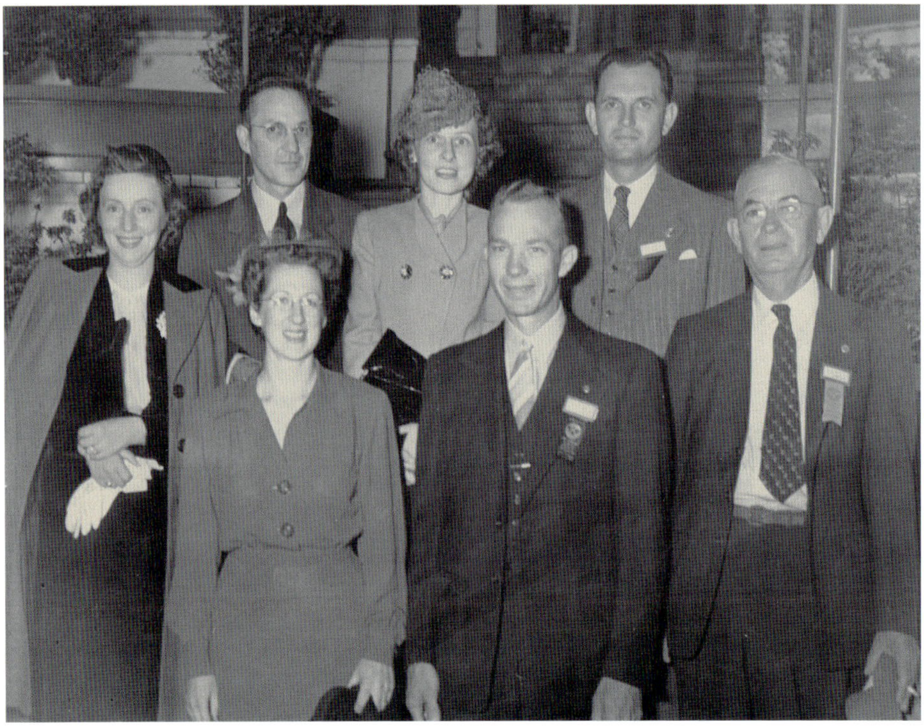

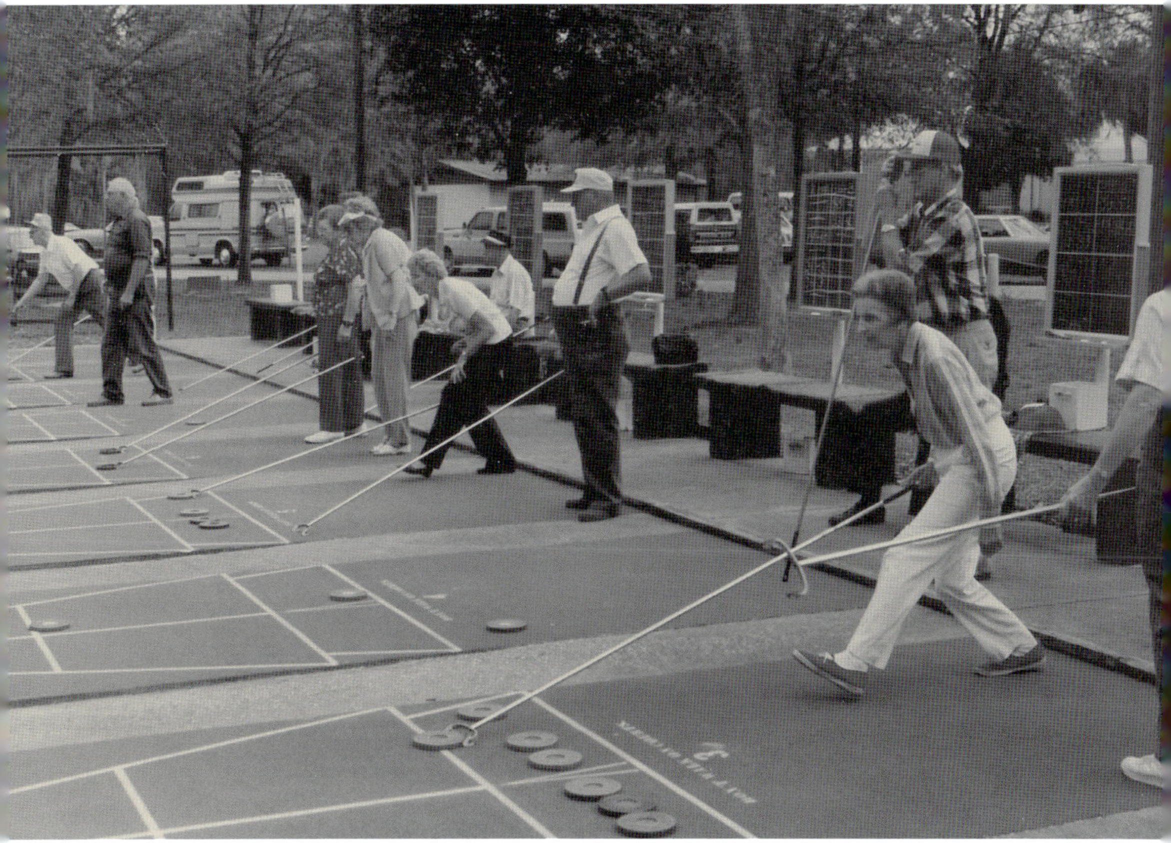

Being located in the central Florida area and having much more sunshine in the winter months than northern neighboring states, Plant City's winter population explodes. This 1990s photograph of the shuffleboard courts at the Winter Visitor Center shows they were quite busy. The recent summer photograph on a very hot day is not as inviting.

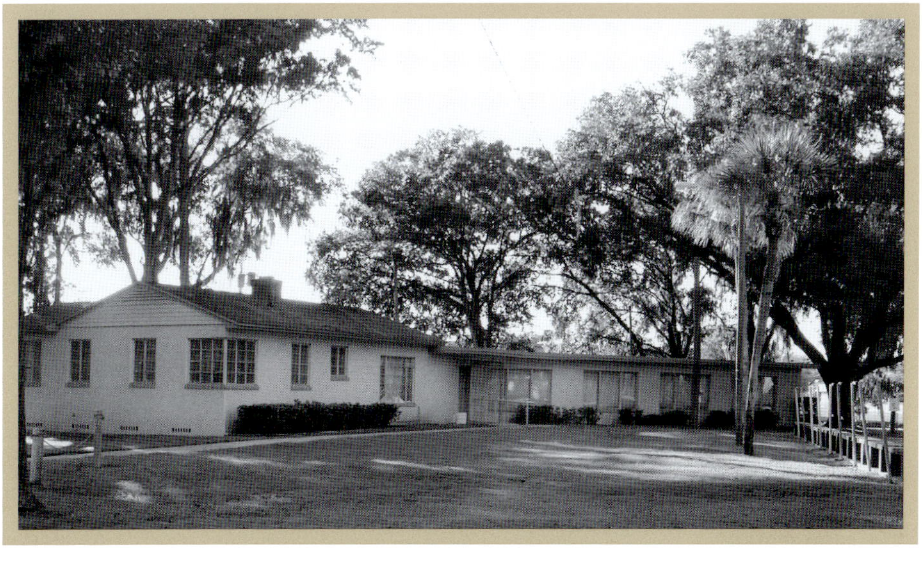

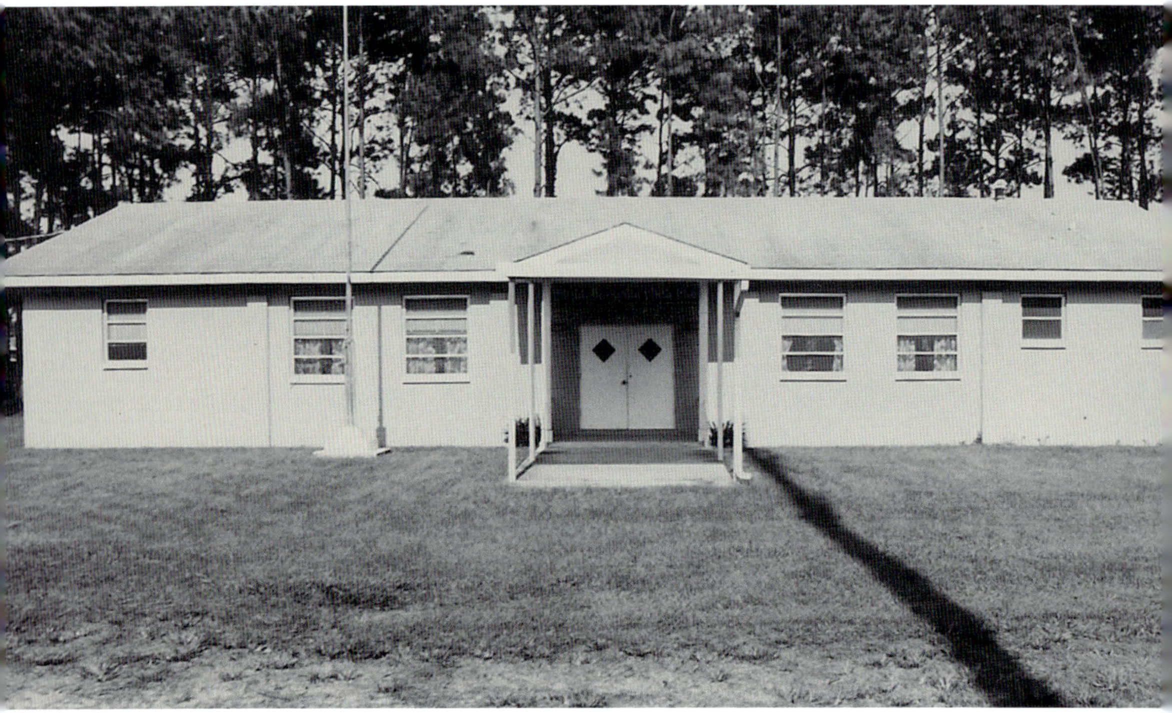

Local residents with Hungarian ancestry felt the need for a clubhouse where they could meet and socialize. They installed the cornerstone for construction of the Magyar Szabadság Kör, or Hungarian Liberty Club, on July 28, 1963. The clubhouse is still used for regular meetings and social gatherings of the descendants and families of those early club members.

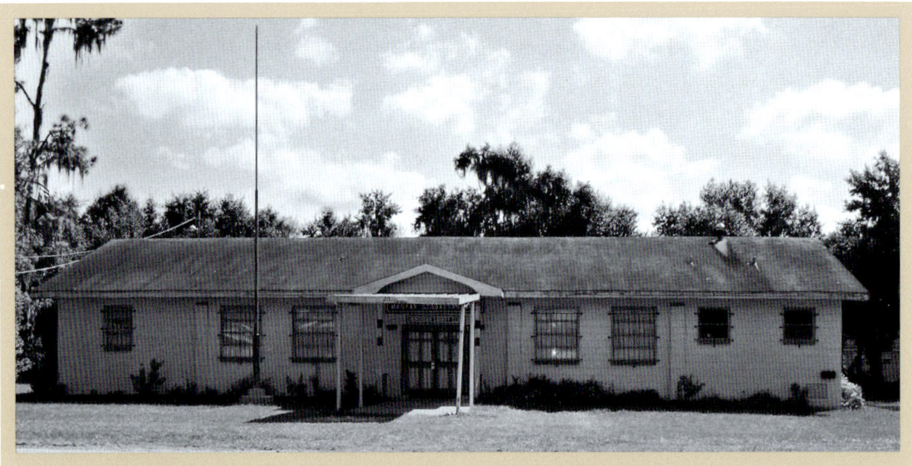

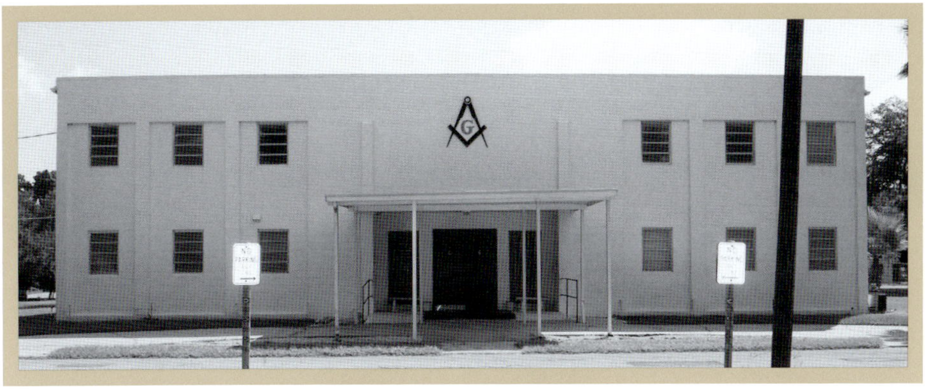

The old wooden Masonic Lodge building that was located at the corner of Mahoney and Evers Streets was destroyed for parking lot expansion in 1958. A newer, more modern concrete block building was built at the apex of West Reynolds Street and Thonotosassa Road. Today the Plant City York Rite, Plant City Order of Eastern Star Chapter 81, and the Olin S. Wright Lodge No. 79 F. and A. M. use the building for their meeting headquarters.

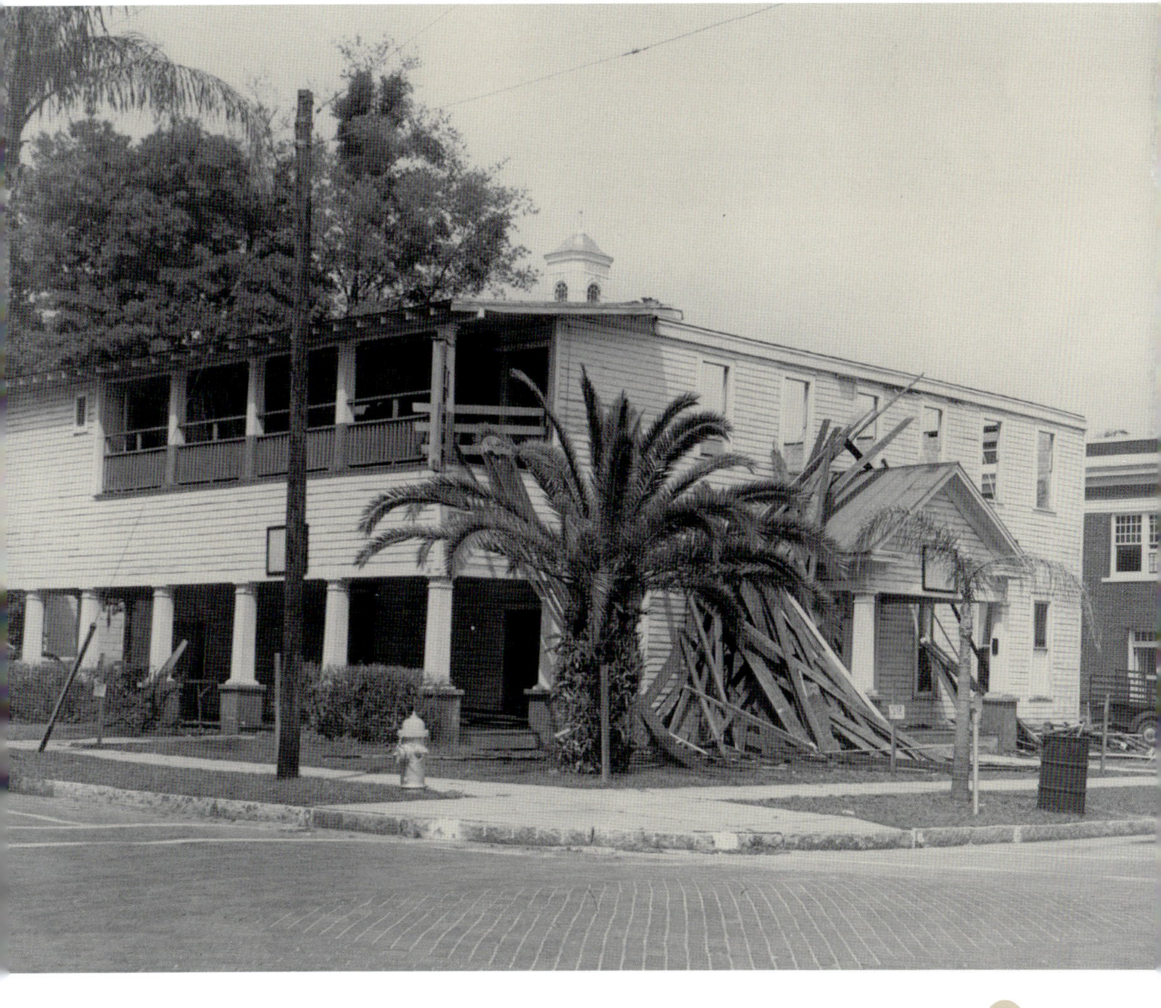

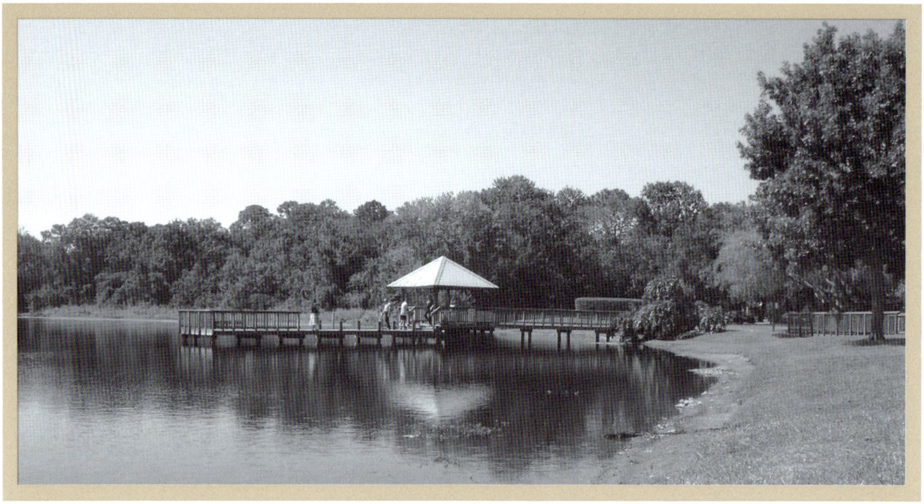

Always known locally as Mud Lake, a 2,000-acre planned unit development, Walden Lake, was designed around this location on the southwestern edge of Plant City in the early 1970s. Bringing a new development of this size was quite a boost to the local real estate market. The gated community includes a 36-hole golf and country club with full-service restaurant and catering facilities in the 27,000-square-foot clubhouse, swimming pools, tennis courts, walking paths, polo fields, and serene settings completing the Walden Lake development. The lakeside gazebo is the site for many family portraits as can be seen in the current photograph. No motorboats are allowed on the lake.

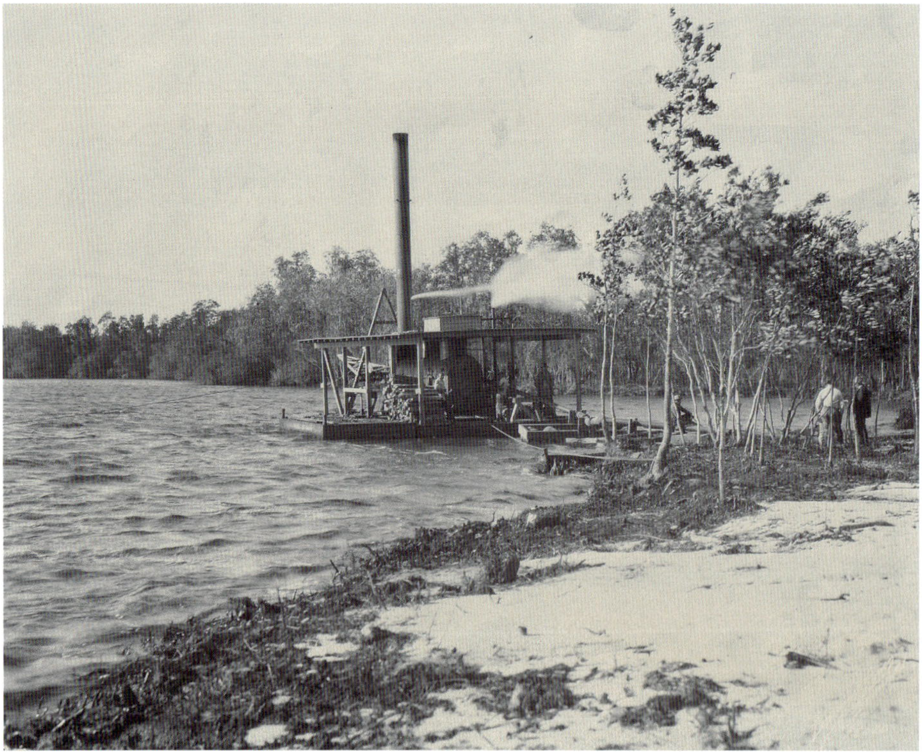

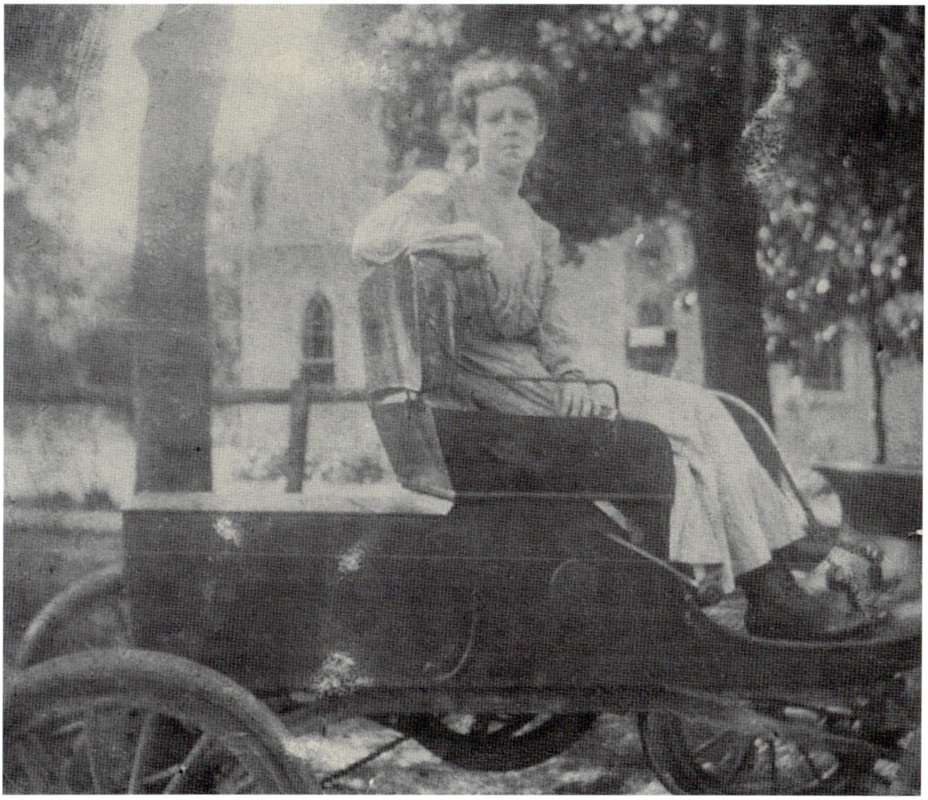

Juno Wright, daughter of Dr. Olin S. Wright, poses in Plant City's first car, an Oldsmobile. The only place gas that could be bought was at his Magnolia Pharmacy. Now antique cars such as this 1927 Ford Model T have been relegated to museums (driver not included). This car is currently exhibited at the historical 1914 Plant City High School Community Center, home of the East Hillsborough Historical Society.

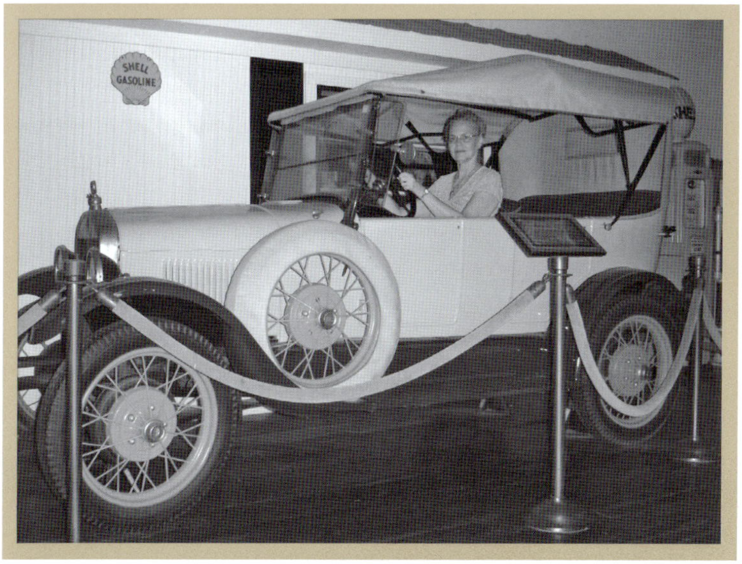

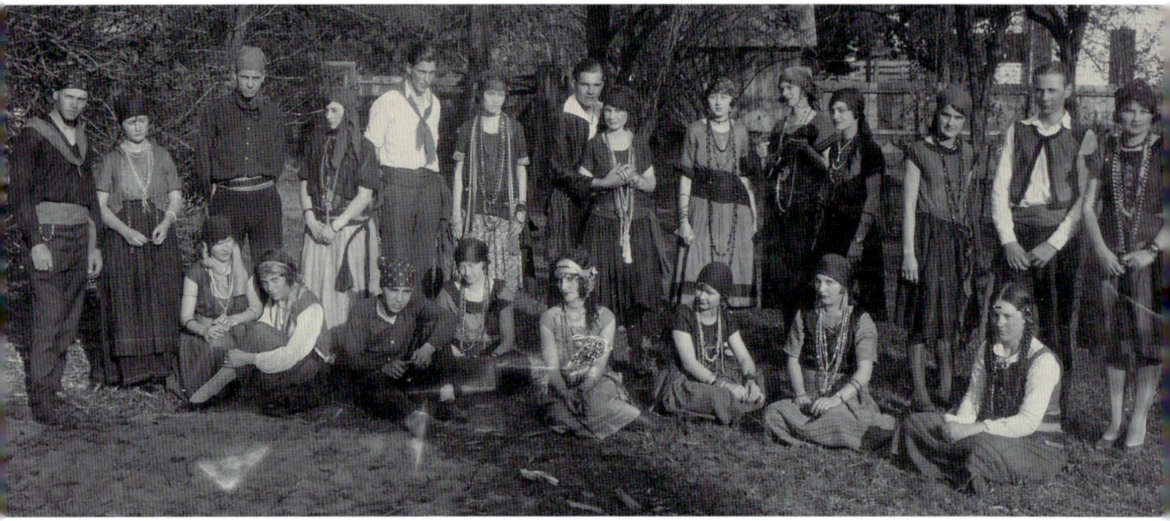

A little drama goes a long way . . . the members of the Plant City High School 1926 class play have a little more serious posture than the young cast of the recent production of *Boyfriend* by Plant City Entertainment.

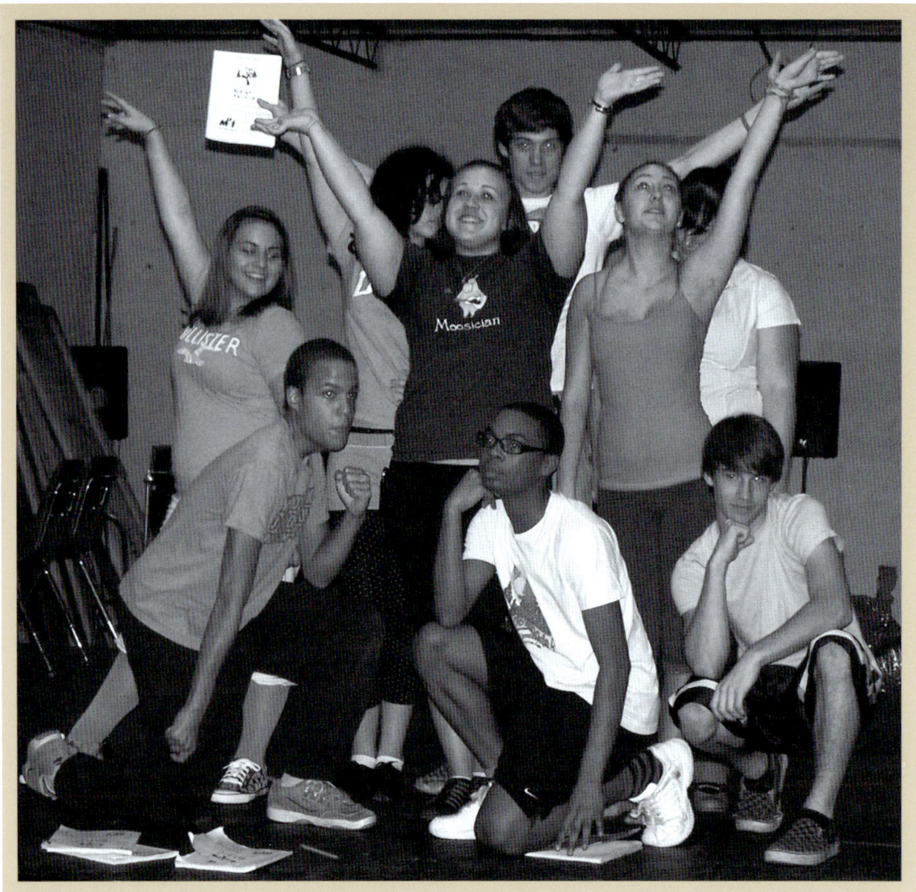

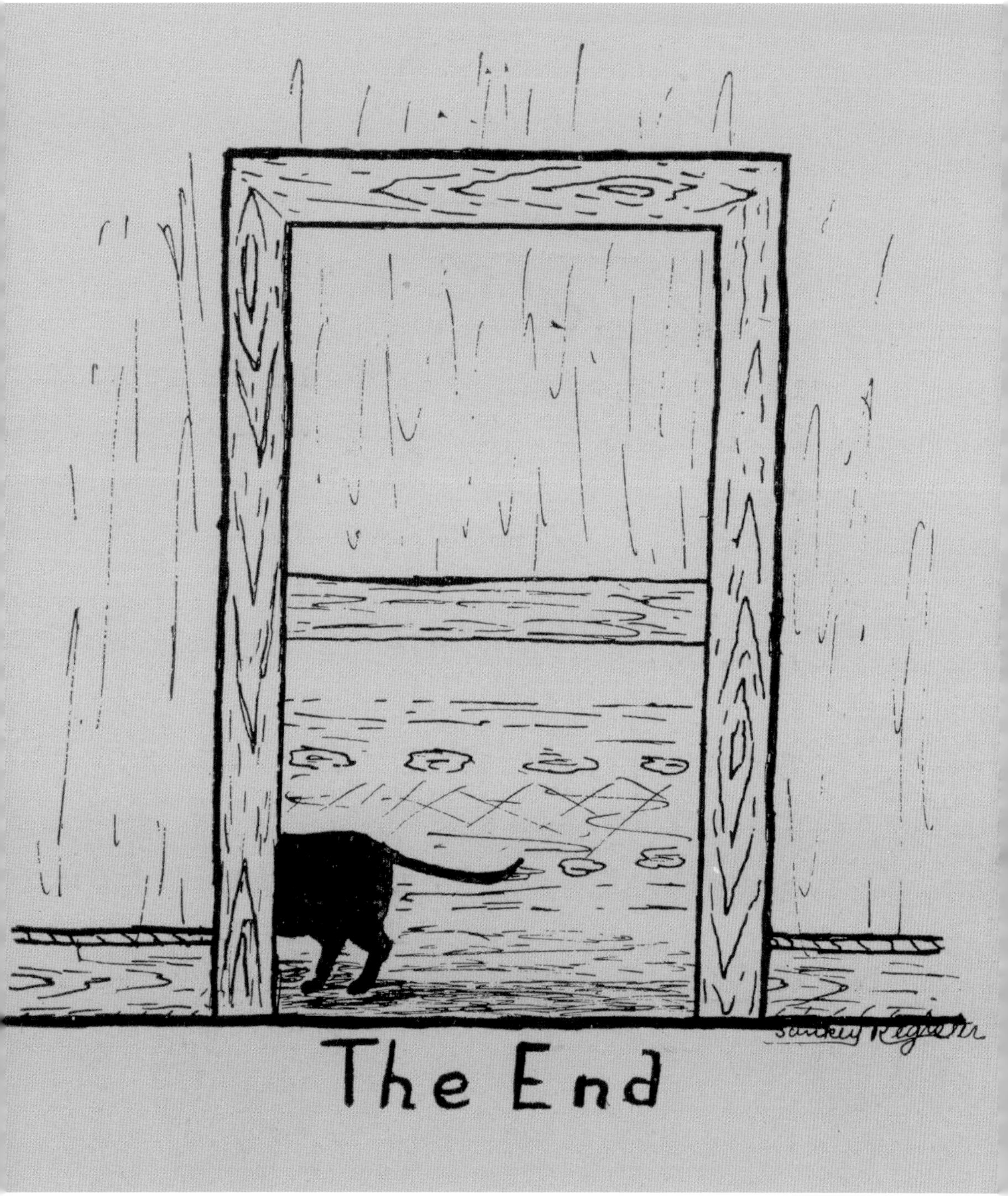

All good things must come to an end, and what better way to end than with artwork by Sankey Register, featured in the 1920 PCHS yearbook *The Kanyuksaw.*